3 WORDS THAT WILL CHANGE YOUR LIFE

*The Secret to Experiencing
the Joy of God's Presence*

MIKE NOVOTNY

BETHANYHOUSE
a division of Baker Publishing Group
Minneapolis, Minnesota

Published by Bethany House Publishers
11400 Hampshire Avenue South
Bloomington, Minnesota 55438
www.bethanyhouse.com

Bethany House Publishers is a division of
Baker Publishing Group, Grand Rapids, Michigan

Printed in the United States of America

Library of Congress Control Number: 2019949901

ISBN 978-0-7642-3528-3

Illustrations by Bethany Vredeveld
Photo of Masada on page 131 © Baker Photo Archive
Cover design by Darren Welch Design

Author is represented by Jones Literary.

20 21 22 23 24 25 26   7 6 5 4

To Kim, Brooklyn, and Maya—
Seeing you each day
reminds me how glorious it will be one day
to see GOD.

Contents

CHAPTER ONE

The Sentence That Can Change Your Life

There is a sentence that can change your life.

It contains just three words and nine letters, yet it is the key to less boredom, more blessing, less rush, more rest, less pacing, more peace, less fear, more faith, less guilt, more grit, less frustration, more satisfaction.

By the way, does that last sentence sound like the start of one of those too-good-to-be-true self-help books? The ones littered with page-turning verbs like "transform" and "revolutionize" and "kick-start"? The ones that promise to divorce-proof your marriage, land you your dream job as a gourmet-donut taste tester, and help you drop thirty pounds without quitting your donut gig?*

This is not that kind of book.

While the sentence is short and simple, the journey it takes you on is lifelong and complex. And though there will be plenty for you to do, this is much more about what Someone else did. Even more, it is about realizing who that Someone else is.

---

*That might be my next book. Because what person would divorce someone who brought home donuts every day?

So, are you ready for it? Take a deep breath, because I am about to tell you the sentence that could change your life.

GOD is here.

I told you! Did you get chills when you read it? Have you already texted your tattoo guy for your first-ever forehead ink? Did you run around the block like an Argentinean soccer announcer, screaming, "GOOOOOOOOOOOOOOOOOOOOOOOD is here!"?

No, not even close?

You don't even have a tattoo guy?

So . . . you just read it like any average sentence?

And your inner grammar nerd was very disappointed that I left the caps lock on?

Well, I'm glad you're reading this book. You need it as much as I do.

You see, zipping past that sentence is one of the worst things you could ever do to your soul. If even one of those three words is misunderstood, you will waste your life working and dating and studying and striving and spending and selling and planning and pushing to find that temporary something to satisfy your heart's desire for an eternal Someone. Building a life around anything other than that sentence will buy the world's most believable lie: One more whatever (dollar/compliment/"like"/victory/achievement/vacation/kid/cause/experience) will finally be enough. But that lie will keep you always one step away from being content with your current life. That lie will convince you to chase the wind even though you will never catch it.

Most Christians, like me, tend to misread those words in ways that rob us of the "full life" that Jesus came into the world to give (John 10:10). In other words, getting this sentence wrong will lead to a half-full life or a barely there life or no life at all. According to Jesus, messing up those three words can kill you.

Here are a few of the most deadly examples of what I mean. You might misread that sentence as . . .

Life Killer #1: *god is here*

Spiritual Life Killer #1

When we replace GOD with god—some generic, run-of-the-mill supernatural being, like "the universe" or a vague "higher power" —we miss the spiritual adrenaline rush of our Father's glorious presence. We yawn while we say his sacred name, deceived by the normality of the letters. As a result, our hearts treat GOD like the yard-care guys who go door-to-door, the ones we wish would just leave us alone so we could get back to binge-watching *The Office*.

We all know the power and immediacy of *here*. When something exciting or thrilling or beautiful or long awaited is at last here, our emotions change even if our situation does not. We get excited and temporarily forget about our fears. We run to the mailbox without bothering to put on our shoes, as if the driveway were holy ground.

But most people don't have that reaction to GOD because they forget to mentally turn on the caps lock. Instead, GOD becomes god—small, unexceptional, uninteresting. His name conjures up memories of being shushed in church and silenced with a ziplock full of Cheerios. Some have confused GOD with some distant universe that we can't talk to but is tracking our daily karma. Others have felt suffocated by some white-bearded, cosmic judge whose only job was to catch and condemn us when we had sex without a ring on our finger.

How about you? When you hear that name, G-O-D, what pops into your mind? Where on your personal list of most exciting thoughts does GOD rank? High enough to spike your spiritual happiness, even if the circumstances of your life don't change?

Your answers to those questions might be why you never were that passionate about the Christian faith. Or why you haven't regularly gone to church since the days when your mom forced you to. Or why you don't care all that much about what the Good Book calls a "GOD-pleasing life." Someone showed you a cheap imitation of GOD, an uninteresting god, and you had better things to do. Someone or something else seemed way more intriguing, so you ran after it instead of running after him.

If all I had seen was a god like that, I would have done the same thing.

Back in the mid-1900s, author A. W. Tozer chastised pastors who shrunk GOD into a mere god: "The poor little undersized, small-minded preacher gets up and begins to chatter about a God he has made in his own image, and then I'm supposed to want to go to heaven and sit beside the throne of a God I could not respect on earth?"[1]

In other words, who cares about heaven if only god lives there?

Many Christians make a similar, but not so blatant, mistake with the sentence I shared with you. They may capitalize the first letter of his name, turning god into God, but their hearts stop far short of the emotional reaction he deserves. They use all the right words to describe him—all-knowing, all-powerful, ever-present, holy—but their familiarity breeds an unintentional contempt.

I once surveyed a group of about fifty Christian teenagers, the vast majority of whom had not only grown up in church but had over a decade of Christian education. For ten school years, Monday to Friday, they had read the Scriptures, gone to chapel, memorized Bible passages, and sung songs like "Holy, Holy, Holy! Lord God Almighty!" If you gave them a quiz, they could have easily checked the right boxes to describe GOD.

But I asked them a simple question: "What would make this year the happiest year of your life?"

Their answers came back as fast as the smiles spread across their faces: "Graduating with honors." "Getting to the playoffs for baseball." "An acceptance letter from my top choice college." "Making the JV2 football team."

Do you know whose name wasn't mentioned by those fifty young Christians? Not one single time? GOD's.[*]

Apparently, in the day-to-day routine of practices and pop quizzes, not one of those Christians thought that GOD was the right place to find lasting joy and the confidence that every teenager craves.

I can't throw stones, though, because I do that too. I know all the right theological words to describe GOD, but I forget the weight of his name so quickly. In the blur of making breakfast, returning emails, and battling the army of weeds attacking my yard, I end up with an orthodox God but not a glorious GOD.

The results of turning off the caps lock are tragic. Happiness deflates. Joy leaks. Peace goes missing. Love grows stale. Confidence hides. Contentment stays home. Satisfaction seems like a myth. Heaven quits being worth it. Repentance seems like a raw deal. Sin seems so much better. Life ends up lifeless. Death gets back its sting.

When someone tries to comfort us with the Bible's best promise, "Don't be afraid. GOD is here!" we brush it off with, "I know, but . . ." Our hearts ache for something, because we've shrunk Someone.

But what if we remember just how truly big GOD is, a GOD so awe-inspiring that his presence makes every other blessing unnecessary for our peace, hope, and joy? What if we cured that slow leak in our hearts by magnifying, exalting, acclaiming, praising, proclaiming, and lifting up the name of GOD every hour of every day? After all, this practice is what Jesus meant when he talked about "hallowing" GOD's name.

Imagine how our lives would be different if God became GOD to us, far and away the best example of every character trait you love in people. The most glorious, forgiving, friendly, strong, smart, pure, patient, powerful, accepting, including, honest, encouraging, compassionate, creative, kind, thrilling, adventurous,

---

[*] In their defense, a fifteen-year-old me would have defined happiness as an inexhaustible Taco Bell gift card.

exciting, inspiring person you could fathom. What if we saw every funny, thrilling, relaxing, interesting, camera-worthy moment in life as an invitation to remember "GOD is even better than this!"?

Then we would have to keep the caps lock on.

Then our God would turn into GOD.

Then the promise of his presence would change our lives.

Life Killer #2: *GOD will be here*

Spiritual Life Killer #2

A second way to miss the power of that sentence is to think of GOD's presence as something that *will be* instead of something that already *is*.

I noticed this when I listened to another group of teenagers who publicly confessed their Christian faith before our church. As part of that celebration, we make short videos where each teen personally answers the question "What does your faith mean to you?"

Want to guess what they said? Kid after kid (after kid after kid) echoed the same words, "My faith means I will go to heaven when I die." After the twelfth kid repeated that answer, I stood up in the back and shouted,* "So GOD doesn't do you any good until you're dead?"†

GOD wants your faith to bless you right here and right now.

---

*Well, I didn't actually stand up and shout anything. I just smiled at the kids, ate cake, and thought of this insightful line long after the event was done.

† And then it dawned on me that we grown-ups were the ones who taught them to see Christianity that way. Ugh.

Faith is more than your FastPass for the Better Place Theme Park. It is not just a key to the pearly gates that you will one day use, but for now just try not to lose.*

Can you imagine if faith only gave you access to GOD in the future? How terrifying would that make today?

Imagine if this glorious GOD was waiting for you then and there but was not present here and now. Imagine going through chemo or a divorce or middle school without him. Imagine trying to deal with the anxiety or heal from the abuse or forgive the friend who betrayed you without GOD at your side. Walking through life's darkest valleys would be terrifying if we tweaked "GOD is here!" to "GOD will be here."

But a GOD-less life is only in the Christian's imagination. Listen to Israel's King David confess his hope in Psalm 23:4, "Even though I walk through the darkest valley, I will fear no evil, for you are with me."

You are. David's fearless life was founded on the present reality of GOD's presence right here, right now.

Of course, there is a distinction between being with GOD here on earth and being with GOD there in heaven. This earth is still broken in hundreds of ways that break our hearts and make us long for the life to come. Heaven is free from clinical anxiety, postpartum depression, social awkwardness, pancreatic cancer, pounding headaches, fake news, petty arguments, and the billions of other proofs that heaven is not a place on earth . . . yet.†

But the greatest part about heaven is available, in part, here and now: the presence of GOD.

The apostle Paul understood this truth: "Rejoice in the Lord always. . . . The Lord is near. . . . And the peace of God, which

---

* To quote comedian Jim Gaffigan, "Am I the only one who finds it odd that heaven has gates? . . . What kind of neighborhood is heaven in?" (From "Jim Gaffigan - Jesus - Beyond the Pale," March 13, 2009, video, https://www.youtube.com/watch?v=2k_9mXpNdgU&list=PL26BC266A3820250B&index=2&t=0s.)

† With all due respect to '80s star Belinda Carlisle.

transcends all understanding, will guard your hearts. . . . I have learned the secret of being content" (Philippians 4:4–5, 7, 12).

Always rejoicing. Hearts guarded by peace. The secret of being content. How is that possible? By believing "the Lord is near." GOD is here!

What if our lives were less of a waiting game and more of a game of hide-and-seek, searching for the GOD who is here but, in part, hidden? What if we sought GOD right now, believing he could be found here, now?

We might end up with more joy.

We might end up with a peace that transcends any situation we may face.

We might end up discovering the secret of being content.

Life Killer #3: *GOD is there*

Spiritual Life Killer #3

The third misreading of this life-changing sentence is that GOD is present but only over there, with other people. We assume that a GOD like that would not want to hang around people like us.

In a way, this lie is logical. Sin has the built-in power to push people apart. Just think of how often this happens in our lives:

- You were best friends, but then she hit on the guy you told her you were into. Now you avoid her offers to go out and grab drinks after class.

14

- You were tight with a co-worker, but then he lied and took all the credit for the project you did together. Now you feel your gut twisting every time his name pops up in your inbox.

- You would love to come home during spring break, but your dad's alcohol addiction has made home where your heart isn't, so you find excuses to stay on campus year-round.

- You were loving your small-group Bible study, but when your private confession became public gossip, you found it hard to go back.

- You felt so close to your spouse, but then you found the search history that proved they had eyes for someone else. Now your heart feels locked away from the one you were meant to be intimate with.

Sin does that. It separates us from each other. And it has the same effect in our relationship with GOD. The Bible puts it like this, "But your iniquities have separated you from your God; your sins have hidden his face from you" (Isaiah 59:2).

A few years ago, a woman who had been regularly attending our church called me to explain why she was not going to be there the following Sunday. "Well, pastor, my ex-boyfriend called the other night and . . . well . . . I know I shouldn't have, but . . ." She went on to explain the temptation she faced and failed to resist.

But her next words were the ones that struck me. "So, obviously, I can't come to church." I asked her to explain the "obviously," since her logic wasn't obvious to me. Her reply, in essence, was, "Because GOD is there."

Feeling far from holy because of her sin, she felt she could not gather around GOD's holy Word with GOD's holy people. She believed her night of short-term pleasure put a long-term pause on her closeness to GOD. Perhaps GOD would want to be there with them, but definitely not here with her.

I wonder if you have ever felt the same way. Perhaps you question, deep in your heart, whether GOD really is here with you. Whether he has stuck around after all you have done. Whether he decided to lock the door to "here" after you messed up for the millionth time. Maybe you think about your own embarrassing behavior—the drinking, the promiscuity, the lack of courage in sharing your faith, the endless desire to be right, the controlling behavior in your relationships, the snap judgments about people's motives, the natural ability to disrespect anyone in authority, the people-pleasing insecurity, the lack of self-control with spending, the critical spirit toward your sister, the pick-and-choose approach to the Christian commandments, the years without prayers (besides the ones for GOD to bail you out of trouble), the years of going through the motions at church, the lack of love for your enemies, the lack of love for GOD. Maybe all of that has left you with a nagging suspicion that GOD is over there with those people and no longer right here with the person you see in the mirror.

This might seem unchristian of me to say, but, in a sense, I am happy that you feel that way. It proves that you believe in GOD. Not in an indifferent, unjust, impotent, shrug-of-the-shoulders god who is too busy styling his long white beard to care deeply about your decisions. Your fear suggests you believe in a holy, righteous, radiant GOD who cares immensely about your sin, because he cares immensely about the people you have sinned against—even when the person you've sinned against is yourself.

There are worse things than feeling ashamed about shameful things you have done.

However, I don't want you to get stuck there, because GOD is much more than a sin hater. He is also a sinner lover. He is not some Santa God who's keeping a list of who's naughty and nice, or some Karma God who "helps those who help themselves." He is a GOD of grace, of undeserved love given to the undeserving. Grace given to the woman who didn't feel worthy to come to worship. Grace given to a man like me who has messed up so much, so many times. Grace given to the sinner you see every time you

16

brush your teeth. This is the grace that gets us from there to here. This is the love that tells sin to pack its bags so that we can check in to the place where GOD *is*. And, because grace is grace, we will never have to leave.

What if we believed that? What if we felt this truth deep in our hearts?

We might discover a GOD who saved us while we were yet sinners.

We just might begin to understand this thing called grace and, better yet, live it out.

We might grasp the true power of true love.

In the final section of this book, I want to prove that Jesus was passionate about getting you into GOD's presence. He lived, died, and rose so that this sentence could be true not just for them, but also for you: GOD is here! The Bible has dozens of ways to say it (saved, forgiven, redeemed, reconciled, justified, born-again, etc.), but every word about Jesus' work leads to the same stunning conclusion. There is no more distance between you and GOD. No more "there."

For every last Christian, the struggling *you* included, GOD is here!

And since GOD is here, so is unfailing love for you, unwavering friendship with you, constant affirmation over you, continual purpose in you, abiding acceptance of you, and never-ending community alongside you. The very things your heart craves are found in the ever-present GOD who is *here*.

The Psalm That Saved Me

Though I had followed Jesus for decades, I had somehow missed the life Jesus died to give me. It was right there in my Bible, in the songs my church sang, in the lectures my professors gave, but I missed it. Until I met Asaph.

Asaph was the singer-songwriter who wrote Psalm 73, an ancient song of worship from the Old Testament. His lyrics are surprisingly transparent. He admitted how angry he felt that the lives of people who did not follow GOD's rules flourished while he suffered. His thoughts were so bitter that he called himself "a brute beast" (v. 22).

But then something changed. Asaph remembered to think much of GOD—to revere GOD. Out of the overflow of his enlightened heart, he sang the words that sent me on a spiritual journey that continues to this day. Asaph asked, "Whom have I in heaven but you?" (v. 25).

That sentence stunned me. When Asaph thought of heaven, he didn't first think of being reunited with loved ones. He thought of GOD. A GOD so good that he made heaven, well, heavenly.

But Asaph wasn't done. He continued, "And earth has nothing I desire besides you" (v. 25).

Asaph's One Wish

That sentence doubled my stunned-ness. Asaph didn't desire romance or fame or achievements or anything, apparently, besides GOD. How could that be? Didn't his heart desire the things of this world? Doesn't yours? Doesn't mine?

Actually no. We don't really desire things of this world, because none of us longs for what fails in the end. We don't want temporary love or friendship that falls apart after a few months. We want something that lasts. We desire what endures forever.

Like . . . GOD.

Asaph's desires taught me something about my own heart. Namely, that I would never be satisfied with temporary blessings. I would always crave more. Or fear that I would end up with less. Nothing short of the eternal GOD would be enough for my soul.

Asaph then affirmed my conclusion, "My flesh and my heart may fail, but God is the strength of my heart and my portion forever" (v. 26).

Where did Asaph find his strength? Simply from being with GOD. And since that portion would last forever, Asaph discovered the source of unquenchable joy.

With the secret of contentment now known, Asaph busted out into a happy dance and invited you to join him in his joy, "But as for me, it is good to be near God" (v. 28).

To be near GOD is so good. It is so good to know GOD is here.

This psalm saved me from sitting around, waiting to die, and riding the sickening roller coaster of life's circumstances. Instead, I learned how to get up and go after GOD, how to seek him until I saw him, which led me to find satisfaction in him. With GOD in mind, I reread the entire Bible, highlighting every word, phrase, and passage about GOD.

I nearly bled my highlighter collection dry.[*]

The theme was everywhere in the Word—GOD's name, GOD's glory, GOD's holiness. Earthly adjectives like "failing" and "temporary" contrasted with divine descriptions like "enduring" and "everlasting." I saw how the commands to praise, magnify, worship, exalt, lift up, and glorify GOD all urge us to ditch our dinky versions of god and think much, much more highly of GOD. I

---

[*] Having a highlighter collection is required for getting your gold card in Bible nerdery.

noticed the descriptions of heaven (GOD is here!) and hell (GOD is not here). I began to hear the drumbeat of joy and gladness that is constantly connected to GOD's presence. I started to value the security and safety of hiding our happiness behind the rock-solid walls of GOD, our refuge and rock and tower and fortress and stronghold and hiding place. I discovered the invitation—for both those new to the faith and those who are longtime followers of Jesus—to seek GOD, see GOD, and know GOD more than ever before.

And when I closed my Bible, I started to hear the same theme everywhere in the world—I opened my eyes and ears to popular culture and heard them—so many of them!—aching for GOD. From Kendrick Lamar to Katy Perry, Alexander Hamilton to Tom Brady, *The Greatest Showman* to *Lego Friends*. Everyone, everywhere was searching for the same thing—to find something as good as GOD that would be as constantly present as GOD promised to be.

The connections between Scripture and culture were so many that I struggled to verbalize what I had found. Even my wife admitted, "I think I know what you are saying, but . . ." Like spaghetti strands stuck to each other, every idea was glued to the next, and I couldn't separate them enough to help others digest the dish. Summarizing Asaph's idea was like asking an elderly man on his sixtieth wedding anniversary to "take ten seconds and tell us how you feel about your wife."

After a few bumbling attempts to get others excited about this book,* I ended up with a one-word elevator pitch—GOD! This book is essentially about GOD. But I'd say that last word in an abnormal way, with bright eyes and a broad smile and outstretched arms. "My book is about . . . GOD!" I knew I was getting closer when a co-worker heard my answer and replied, "GOD? Like with the caps lock on?"

---

* Which ended with glazed eyes and forced smiles and "Wow, that sounds . . . um . . . interesting. I'll have to read that."

Exactly. This book is not about god or God. It's about GOD! And that GOD is here!

That sentence has changed me. It still is changing me. Admittedly, I have a long way to go. My soul deals with its own dementia, and I think too little of GOD's presence too often. But, day by day, the Holy Spirit is opening my eyes to the glorious GOD who is with me always. My highs have gotten much higher and longer and my lows are much shorter and not as low. And I have found life—abundant, amazing life. I have tasted and seen, and I swear that the Lord is good.

I want more of it. More of him. Much more.

That is where I want to take you in this book. I want to open your eyes to the Scriptures that have always been right there in front of you but that you might have missed. And I want to connect more of your daily experiences to the divine, so that your synapses send a thousand push notifications to your soul. GOD is here.

In the end, I pray that both of us can join Asaph in his astounding claim that there is only one thing we truly desire. And that thing is not far, far away, unreachable, and impossible. Through the love of our Father, the sacrifice of his Son, and the work of his Spirit, that thing is as close as your breath.

I pray you will start to think the greatest thought—GOD is here!

Life Giver: GOD Is Here!

Recently, three sad kids from my church experienced a glimpse of the joy that sentence brings into our lives. Their mom was serving in the military, stationed on the other side of the earth about eight time zones away from here. Like most kids in their situation, they missed her intensely and counted down the days until her return.

Little did they know, Mom had planned a surprise.

One day, on a visit to Grandpa's house, the kids walked in and gasped at the giant gift-wrapped box in the living room, big enough to hide a hundred stuffed animals. Family members who were in on the surprise got out their phones as the kids tore open the gift and discovered . . . Mom!

Can you picture their three little faces as they threw their arms around Mom's neck? Can you feel their joy as they pressed their noses against hers? Can you hear them squealing, "Mommy is here!"?

The presence of the right person changed everything.

In the pages to come, I invite you to join me on a journey to unwrap the ultimate present Jesus died and rose to give you. Or, to put it in a single sentence, I invite you to put your hope in the promise that . . .

GOD is here.

STUDY QUESTIONS

1. Which of the three "life killers" resonated the most with you? Explain your answer to a Christian friend.

2. When you hear the name G-O-D, what pops into your mind? If you had to give your mental image of GOD a letter grade (with A-plus being as exciting as it gets), which grade would your GOD get?

3. Read Psalm 73, the ancient song that sent me on a journey to find GOD. List all the connections you see between this psalm and the main points of this chapter.

PART 1

GOD _____ .

CHAPTER TWO

Our Biggest Problem and GOD's Bigger Solution

We don't think that much of GOD.

That is our biggest problem. We might have plenty of problems, but this is the problem beneath the problems, the polluted spring that produces the water that keeps making us emotionally sick. The toxic seed that keeps producing poisonous fruit. The crippling fear of getting dumped by your boyfriend or downsized by your company or diagnosed by your doctor only exists because we don't think that much of GOD.

I'm not being holier-than-thou, because this is my problem too. When an unplanned car repair sends me into an anxiety spiral or a flopped sermon leads to self-loathing on a Sunday night, my real issue is that I don't think much of GOD.

That problem is true in two different ways—quantity and quality. We don't think that much of GOD because we don't think about him often enough (quantity). And we don't think that much of GOD because our thoughts about him are, frankly, pretty lame (quality).

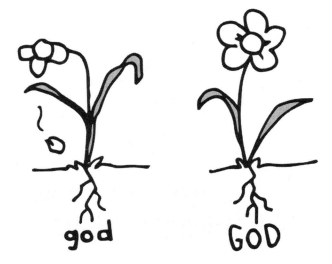

A Picture of Your Biggest Problem?

Think of the times when your thoughts gravitate toward GOD. You might bring up his name when you "say grace" before a family dinner. Or maybe you talk to GOD as you stare at your bedroom ceiling at night. You might mention GOD at a church or in a hospital waiting room.

Our brains make a synaptic connection between certain places (dinner tables, bedsides, churches) and the presence of GOD. But here's the issue—we might only spend 1 percent of our week in those places. Which means we don't think of GOD 99 percent of the time.

The quantity of that percentage is a problem.

What is more, even when you are thinking *about* GOD, you probably don't think that much *of* GOD. Your thoughts of him might be as thrilling as getting a case a rice cakes for your birthday.*

---

* If the thought of getting rice cakes excites you, you need more help than this book is capable of providing.

26

For example, have you ever mindlessly talked to GOD before a meal, saying all the right words but having a heart that is far from floored at the fact that GOD is with you?

My family often says a dinner prayer that starts, "Come, Lord Jesus, be our guest," which should blow our minds. *Jesus is our guest?! The Lord himself is showing up for pesto ravioli?! GOD is here?!* But sadly, our minds are rarely blown by the miracle. Instead we say, "Pass the Parmesan" a mere 0.002 seconds after "Amen," which calls into serious question whether any of us were actually thinking about GOD at all.

Ever been there?

Or have you ever found yourself singing about GOD's love, mercy, and salvation, yet paying more attention to the pitch of the tone-deaf worshiper behind you or the dry scalp of the gentleman ahead of you or the typo on the projector screen in front of you?

Or has some well-meaning Christian ever tried to bring healing to your hurting soul with the reminder, "But GOD is here," and you brushed it off like GOD was no more than a nursing intern and you needed to speak to a real doctor?

If so, welcome to the club. Like me, you are a card-carrying member of the "Don't Think That Much of GOD" society. In both quantity and quality, it is frighteningly easy to think little of GOD.

You're Killin' Me, Smalls god

But thinking so little of GOD is killing us.

I choose the word "killing" carefully. Because death, from a biblical perspective, is separation from life, and life is what you get to enjoy when you think much of GOD.

Let me unpack that last sentence.

Life, in the Bible's terms, is what you experience when you are with GOD. When you receive what Jesus came to give, that massive GOD-shaped hole in your heart is filled with never-ending love, continual community, 24/7 purpose, guaranteed acceptance, enduring happiness, and all the other stuff your soul constantly craves. Find GOD and you have found life.

To put it more simply, the only biblical way to "live" is to believe GOD is here!

Death Defined

Think of it like this picture: The larger circle is GOD as he actually is—glorious, satisfying, enough. The smaller circle is GOD as you think of him. And the space in between these two circles is death.

Death is the feeling that your current life is not enough. Or the fear that you will lose the thing you need to survive. Or the worry that you'll end up without the one person who makes life worth living. Discontentment lives in the space between the circles, along with its whining roommates, hopelessness and dissatisfaction.

The less we think of GOD, the more painful our daily death.

There is only one solution that will satisfy your soul—to think much of GOD.

Which is why we need to fully grasp what the name of GOD actually means.

Nothing Matters More Than GOD's Name

What's in a name?

Shakespeare tried to answer that question with his famous lines about the roses in Romeo's garden. When it comes to someone's name, what matter more than the sounds your mouth makes are the thoughts your mind thinks.

Because a "name" is what you think about when you think about that name.

Just ask my fifth-grade friends. Back in the early '90s, I went to school with twin sisters who every boy thought were drop-dead cute.* None of us eleven-year-olds knew a thing about love, romance, or relationships, but we knew the names of those girls. We brought up their names during second recess. We circled their names in our yearbooks. We repeated their names at our sleepovers. In fact, I remember mentioning their names in my bedtime prayers!

My fifth-grade faith was so strong that I even prayed, "You can pick either one to be my girlfriend, GOD. Your will be done!"†

Those two names were much more than a mash-up of consonants and vowels. For the boys at school, the names of those girls brought to mind their personalities, their talents, and their admirable characters.‡

The same is true for any name. For example, when I say the name Aaron Rodgers, our minds do much more than spell. They instinctively react. Packers fans chant, "MVP!" while Bears fans growl in response to decades' worth of NFC frustration.§ When I say the name Tupac, hip-hop lovers put their hands in the air

---

*If you happen to be one of those sisters, I apologize for this rather awkward section of the book.

†I know, I know. My submission to the will of GOD was an admirable example for us all.

‡I know that sentence is not the whole truth, but listing the thoughts and motivations of fifth-grade boys seemed unwise.

§If, at the time of your reading this book, the Bears are better than the Packers, please know we are living in the end times.

while grandmothers wrinkle their foreheads (unless your grandmother is a West Coast gangster). If I mention your dad's name, your face might light up or tense up. The same name can cause joy or fear, relief or anxiety, anticipation or indifference. Because a person's name is the sum total of all the thoughts you think about them.

But that's the funny thing about names. They are not objective. There is not one thing that everyone thinks when they hear any given name. There is not a mutually agreed-upon feeling for every name we hear. Names are subjective.

The Name Game

So, what do you think when I say this name: GOD?

What thoughts flood your mind when you hear his name? What feelings fill your heart? Did you smile? Sing? Shrug? Please don't read another paragraph until you have thought about what you think about GOD.

If our response to the name of GOD is not all that positive, that's probably why reading the Bible is so difficult for many of us. After all, the thrilling story of the Bible is that Jesus came to be with us so that we could be with GOD. But what if GOD isn't all that thrilling?

30

Then heaven might seem boring, hell not so bad, contentment too good to be true, satisfaction a wish to only be dreamed of, fear inevitable, lasting happiness unattainable, obedience too high a price, repentance out of the question, peace nearly impossible, the cross maybe avoidable, sin perhaps preferable, community unnecessary, and Christianity . . . optional.

But if you think much of GOD, heaven becomes indescribable, hell unthinkable, contentment doable, satisfaction reachable, fear optional, happiness attainable, obedience doable, repentance preferable, peace possible, the cross bearable, sin treatable, community a necessity, and Christianity a no-brainer.

What Matters More Than Starvation and Salvation

Early in his three-year teaching career, Jesus' followers approached him with a request. They asked for a tutorial: "Lord, teach us to pray" (Luke 11:1).

And, as you might expect, Jesus encouraged them to pray for "daily bread" (v. 3), the stuff we need to make it through the day— food, drink, clothing, housing, safety, etc.

Jesus also urged them to pray for forgiveness, both received and given. "Forgive us our sins, for we also forgive everyone who sins against us" (v. 4). We all need GOD to send our sins away, to delete the offensive things we have done. And we need GOD to motivate us to love the people who have not loved us, so we don't exact payback and blow up the peace in our homes, workplaces, and neighborhoods.

These are massively important prayers, right? Without daily bread, we starve. Without forgiveness, we can't be saved.

But did you notice anything about the quotes? I skipped a verse. Before verse three's daily bread and verse four's forgiveness comes verse two, the start of our Lord's prayer. Apparently, Jesus believed something mattered even more than starvation and salvation.

31

GOD's name.

Jesus teaches, "When you pray, say: 'Father, hallowed be your name'" (v. 2). What Jesus wants you to pray about, before anything else, is the hallowing of GOD's name.

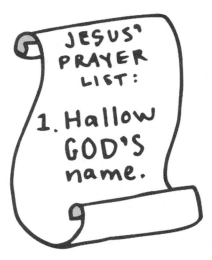

Jesus' Prayer List

Which would be so powerful . . . if we only knew what "hallowed" meant!

Besides Halloween and perhaps the Deathly Hallows of Harry Potter, we are not too familiar with that word. I wonder how many Christians pray that prayer without a clue what the first line actually means!

Let's put the prayer into everyday language so we don't miss Jesus' point:

- "Hallowed" means to see something as holy.
- "Holy" means something set apart or different (in a wonderful way).
- "Your name" refers to the thoughts we have when we think about GOD.

Put it all together and Jesus is teaching us to pray, "Father, let my thoughts about you be wonderfully different." Or, as I like to think of it, "GOD, let me think much of you today."

That line is the key to Jesus' prayer, the truth that makes the rest of the requests make sense. Why would I want GOD's will to be done unless I thought of GOD as wonderfully different from me—smarter, wiser, and more qualified to call the shots? Why would I want to be forgiven if forgiveness only gave me access to a lame, uninteresting, boring god? Why would I care about temptation and sin unless GOD was so good that offending him would be truly offensive? Why would I offer him all the glory if he wasn't all that glorious?

The whole prayer hangs on that first request—GOD, let me think much of you today.

That line is so powerful that I rarely finish praying Jesus' prayer. I have a six-minute drive from my home to my workplace, and (on my more spiritual days) I like to pray the Lord's Prayer on my commute. So, I begin, "Father, hallowed be your name."

But then I pause and try to think much of GOD. I think about how wonderful GOD must be if he is better than the best things in my life. I look at the beauty of the leaves changing colors on Appleton Street and imagine how breathtaking GOD must be. I remember the love of my daughters as they smoosh their little noses against mine before going to school and try to fathom how GOD could love me more than I love them. I think about how good I felt devouring those microwaved sausage patties at breakfast* and dream about how much better it is to spend today in the presence of GOD.

As I drive, I try to hallow his name. I try to think much of GOD, so much that his name becomes wonderful enough to comfort me no matter what lies ahead. I remember that while the morning kisses and processed pork patties gave me a temporary high, GOD is my portion forever.

Most of the time, I pull into my parking spot before I'm done hallowing his name. I might squeeze in the rest of Jesus' prayer on

---

* Judge not, y'all. Sausage patties are one of GOD's greatest gifts.

my way from my car to the front door. But I don't mind. Because Jesus has helped me think much of GOD. He has helped me to think of GOD as wonderfully different.

Which is all my heart needs for the day.

Maybe you could visualize that part of the Lord's Prayer as the solution to the problem we illustrated above. We said that death is the difference between GOD as he is and god/God as we picture him. Fear, worry, and despair have free rein when our GOD is forgettably small.

Hallowed Be Your Name

Jesus' prayer essentially asks GOD to loan you a spiritual air pump, to stick a needle into his name and blow it up, thought by thought, until your faith gets closer and closer to the truth. The more his name is hallowed, the more wonderful and frequent our thoughts of GOD become, the more Asaph's soul-satisfying desire becomes our own—all I want today is GOD! And the less chance fear has to overwhelm our hearts.

Which is what the Ten Commandments remind us to do too.

What Matters More Than Murder and Adultery

Do you think Moses questioned GOD when he read the original version of the Ten Commandments?

34

I like to think of Moses reading the tablets for the very first time, stroking his beard, and nodding in affirmation. "'No other gods.' That's a good place to start, GOD. 'Honor your father' is top five for sure. I can't wait to share that with my kids!* 'You shall not murder or commit adultery or steal or give false testimony.' GOD, I have to say these are really good.

"But . . . can I offer one humble suggestion, Lord? That part about 'you shall not misuse the name of the Lord'. . . well, not to be presumptuous, but it feels a touch out of order. I mean, top three commandments? You want people to think about that before the stuff about murdering a cheating ex or sleeping with a neighbor's wife? Maybe we could bump the name thing back to the coveting section near the end. But overall, GOD, really solid job."†

And if Moses had really said all this, I would have agreed with him. I mean, I would much rather have someone misuse GOD's name than murder someone in my family. And I can deal with some profanity much easier than I can handle people's lies, gossip, and slander.

But GOD didn't wait to talk about his name. Right there near the top of the list we find "You shall not misuse the name of the LORD your God, for the LORD will not hold anyone guiltless who misuses his name" (Exodus 20:7).

Doesn't quite seem like top ten material, does it?

Unless you remember that everything is in *that* name.

As I will explain in the pages to come, the reason we break the commandments about violence and sex and stealing is that we have first broken the commandments about GOD and his name. Without a massively glorious GOD to make us happy and deal with our discontentment, we reach for anyone and anything to fill that void in our hearts. Even if we have to lie about her. Or sleep with him. Or talk back to Mom and Dad.

---

* This is where Moses and GOD would have fist-bumped if GOD were a physical being with fists.

† Moses, of course, would have used the Oreo cookie approach when criticizing the Lord, sandwiching his suggestion between two encouraging compliments.

In other words, get GOD's name right, and you'll do the right thing. But misuse his name, and wrongdoing is right around the corner.

Let's unpack exactly what that means.

Misuse and Missed Use

What happens when you misuse GOD's name? When you connect his holy name to things that are less than wonderfully different? What happens in your heart when you habitually toss in his name to flippantly fill sentences or express any random emotion? What is the result?

You water down his name.

And, in the end, you don't think much of GOD.

Which is the biggest problem of all.

Imagine your boss gifted you with a 1992 Screaming Eagle Cabernet for your birthday. You thank her for the oversized bottle of red wine and promise to share it at the upcoming company Christmas party. Later that evening, you Google the label to learn more about the vintage and find that this is one of the most expensive wines in the world. Sold at a charity event back in 2000, a bottle went for $500,000.

You could buy a lot of dollar menu McChickens with that haul!

Now, imagine that you bring the bottle to the Christmas party. You uncork the Screaming Eagle and pour a few pricey ounces into your Ikea wineglasses. But just when you are ready for the toast and your first sip, Darrell from HR turns on the office tap and sticks his glass underneath the lukewarm water.

You cringe in horror. Your boss lunges for the faucet. Darrell gets some serious daggers from around the room.

Why? Because you don't water down wonderful wine.

The same is true for GOD's name. The pure, unadulterated name of GOD is priceless. It offers more happiness and excitement than anything Napa Valley can offer. Unless you water it down.

36

Stick the name of GOD underneath the faucet of misuses (screaming Jesus' name at an aggressive driver, using his name in vain for any and every reason, etc.), and our heart un-hallows the name of GOD. Our thoughts about his name get connected to stuff that is not wonderful or at all different. His name becomes common. Mundane. Dull.

In a verbal flood of misuses, the name of GOD becomes a drop of expensive wine in an ocean of water. Eventually, his name means little or nothing to our hearts. The promise "GOD is here!" becomes as spiritually satisfying as warm water on a summer day. We become name numb. So callous to the name above every name that we can hear it, say it, and read it with zero emotional response.

Breaking this commandment is like letting all the air out of that inner circle, allowing GOD to become small and uninteresting in our minds and hearts. And once that happens, life leaves and death takes its place.

Which is why, perhaps, before he told us to honor our parents or respect the ring on a co-worker's finger, GOD commanded us to protect his holy reputation.

But there is a more subtle danger contained in the commandment. Many Christians, committed to GOD's top ten list, learn to clean up their language and save his name for prayers and songs of praise. Yet they still end up thinking too little of GOD.

Why? Because the greatest misuse of GOD's name is the missed use of GOD's name.

When a day goes by without much thought of GOD, we have missed a chance to use his name. When we eat breakfast or rock out to "Enter Sandman"* or bust out laughing after a hilarious text or do anything good without thinking about GOD, we have missed the chance to use his name. GOD gave us a slow pitch to consider how wonderful he must be if he is better than breakfast

---

* The Metallica classic that, ironically, includes a prayer for GOD to bless and keep our souls!

37

or music or laughter, but we took the pitch without a swing. We failed to hallow his name.

This was (and still is) my biggest struggle with the commandment. It would take months, maybe years, to catch me dropping a misuse in a conversation. But it would take minutes, maybe seconds, to witness a missed use—a whiff on GOD's name. I have so many chances to taste and see that the Lord is good, but I leave them untouched on my plate.

Which circles back to our original problem: We don't think much of GOD. Either through our misuse (quality) or missed use (quantity) of his name, our GOD becomes someone less, a miniature version of the glorious One who wants to make us the most satisfied people on earth.

This is why GOD tells us a thousand times, in a dozen ways, to think more of his name.

From God to GOD

Have you ever counted how many commands there are from GOD about GOD? The Bible is filled with direct orders to worship, honor, glorify, magnify, praise, remember, and fear GOD. A summation of all these commands is "Think much of GOD!"

If you open a church hymnal or turn on Christian radio, you'll come across certain verbs peppered throughout the lyrics. This is because modern songwriters often draw from the ancient psalms, which urge us to think much about GOD.

Let's take a look at a few:

Worship GOD—To worship means to believe something is of the highest worth. The thing you treasure the most in life is what you worship. The thing you would sacrifice anything to keep is what you worship. The opinion that means the most to you comes from the person you worship. When Christians claim to worship GOD, we are saying that GOD is worth more than everything and everyone else in our lives.

Psalm 100 urges us, "Worship the Lord with gladness; come before him with joyful songs" (v. 2). Gladness and joyful songs come from the realization that our glorious GOD is here ("come before him").

Honor GOD—To honor means to hold great admiration and respect for someone. When Christians honor GOD, we are telling the world how much we respect his love, power, and character. We admire him for the salvation Jesus has won for us and for who GOD is by his very nature.

Psalm 22 says, "You who fear the Lord, praise him! All you descendants of Jacob, honor him! Revere him, all you descendants of Israel!" (v. 23). King David, the author of this song, wants to pump up our view of GOD, so he stacks one verb after another—fear, praise, honor, revere! Think much of GOD!

Glorify GOD—To glorify, in the original Hebrew sense of the word, is to say that someone has weight, significance. Even in English we say, "He's a *heavy* hitter" or "She's a *big* deal." When Christians glorify GOD, we express through our words and deeds that GOD is the most significant thing in our lives. He is not like a pop song that will be forgotten by next year. He is the eternal GOD who will be the biggest deal forever and ever!

Psalm 86 sings, "I will praise you, Lord my God, with all my heart; I will glorify your name forever" (Psalm 86:12). The author plans to make GOD's name a big deal for the rest of his life. He wants us to think that much of GOD too.

Praise GOD—To give praise, in the Greek language of the New Testament, literally means "to say something good." The Greek noun is "eulogy," a compound word that puts together "good" and "word." So when you say something nice at Uncle Bob's funeral, you are giving a eulogy. You are, literally, praising him. When Christians praise GOD, we say good things about his actions and character.

The word *praise* is used 182 times in the book of Psalms alone, begging us to say lots of good things about GOD. Psalm 9, for example, says, "I will be glad and rejoice in you; I will sing the praises of your name, O Most High" (v. 2). Notice the connection between praising GOD's name and joy. When we say good things about GOD, what we think of him gets better (his name), and the result is the joyful feeling of gladness that this GOD is here with us!

Remember GOD—To remember something is to recall it and keep it at the forefront of our minds. Since GOD is not visible, letting him be "out of sight, out of mind" is a real tendency for us. Therefore, many Bible passages remind us to remember, to keep "seeing" a glorious, exalted GOD in our thoughts.

Psalm 63 models this kind of remembering: "On my bed I remember you; I think of you through the watches of the night" (v. 6). When David couldn't sleep, he remembered GOD. He thought of GOD's glory, GOD's plans, and GOD's unfailing presence. No wonder praise fills the rest of this psalm!

Fear GOD—One of the most misunderstood biblical phrases, to "fear GOD" does not mean to be horrified of him. In Scripture, fear is often connected to a sense of awe, thinking someone is so awesome that we feel nervous in their presence. If you ran into your favorite actress or athlete at a restaurant, you might experience this type of fear. If you stood a few steps from the edge of the Grand Canyon, you would experience biblical "fear."[*] You would stand in awe. You would be emotionally moved.

Psalm 34 commands, "Fear the LORD, you his holy people, for those who fear him lack nothing" (v. 9). What a promise! If we are in awe of the Lord (that is, we think much of GOD), we'll lack nothing. All the love, acceptance, friendship, and praise that we need is found in the eternal GOD who will always be here with us.

I could go on, but I think you get the point. The entire Bible—including the majority of the Psalms, the Lord's Prayer, and the Ten Commandments—is urging us to think much of GOD. Our Father knows that the human heart has a slow leak and needs to be reminded that GOD is not some small god or some technically correct God; he is GOD!

---

[*] Shout-out to Pastor Nate Wordell for sharing this comparison with me.

So, what does this mean for you? Why do the Scriptures stack the synonyms in song after song?

Answer: So that we will think more of GOD. So we tap into every blessing from the past, every gift of the present, and every promise for the future in order to hallow GOD's name.

That is the essential goal of every day of life. Not to get our to-do lists done. (Unless our to-do lists start with "Think much of GOD!") Not just to get our hands on another short-term burst of happiness. But to leverage every good moment to make his name great.

Seek, See, and Satisfied

The Bible describes thinking much of GOD as a three-step process, which I call Seek, See, Satisfied. It's all about getting such a clear view of GOD that the very sight of him is enough to satisfy our souls. But our souls will never be truly satisfied until we learn to "see" GOD as glorious. And we will never see GOD in that way until we seek him with all our hearts.

This is a huge deal, so let's take each of those steps in turn:

Seek—Seeking is the mental journey our minds take from thinking little of god to thinking much of GOD. It's not like seeking the ocean, where we physically travel from our current location to the nearest coast. It's the patient process of guiding our thoughts closer to the glory of GOD. We can lie in bed or sit in a pew or stand in line at Target and seek GOD.

Consider a few of the Bible's encouragements to seek GOD:

- "Now devote your heart and soul to seeking the LORD your God" (1 Chronicles 22:19).
- "Look to the LORD and his strength; seek his face always" (1 Chronicles 16:11).
- "You, God, are my God, earnestly I seek you" (Psalm 63:1).
- "Glory in his holy name; let the hearts of those who seek the LORD rejoice" (1 Chronicles 16:10).

41

Make no mistake, this is mental CrossFit. If your mind is like mine, there will be a billion squirrels to chase that scurry in every direction except toward GOD. This takes practice, devotion, and earnest effort, as the passages above describe. We don't stumble into GOD's presence. We enter his presence by seeking him.

See—Once we have sought and found GOD, we can see him as he actually is—exalted, glorious, beautiful, captivating, satisfying.

King David writes, "One thing I ask from the LORD, this only do I seek: that I may dwell in the house of the LORD all the days of my life, to gaze on the beauty of the LORD and to seek him in his temple" (Psalm 27:4).

Why does David want to "seek" only the Lord? So he can "gaze" at his face. So he can see GOD.

The glorious reward of seeking is seeing. And the view is stunning. When we gaze at the Lord, we'll glimpse what most religious people never see. We'll see GOD!

Satisfied—The very sight of GOD is the most satisfying thing for our souls.

David connected the dots for us in one of my favorite psalms. "You, God, are my God, earnestly *I seek you*; I thirst for you, my whole being longs for you, in a dry and parched land where there is no water. *I have seen you* in the sanctuary and beheld your power and your glory. Because your love is better than life, my lips will glorify you. I will praise you as long as I live, and in your name I will lift up my hands. *I will be fully satisfied* as with the richest of foods; with singing lips my mouth will praise you" (Psalm 63:1–5, emphasis added).

David is mentally going after GOD like a parched man going after a pool of cool water. Why is David so desperate? Because he has already seen GOD, beheld his glory, and understood what a big deal he is. David had enjoyed many good things in life (praise from an impressed Israel, power as a newly crowned king, friendship from faithful Jonathan), yet GOD's love was better than it all. The richest foods of the palace were good, but being with GOD was better.

He was fully satisfied in the presence of the GOD who is here.

And you can be satisfied too.

Full satisfaction comes from seeing GOD, from getting a twenty-twenty glimpse of his glory. And that glorious sight becomes visible as we seek his face, when we pour mental energy into directing our thoughts to GOD.

Most people are too busy for that. Their schedules have no space for seeking. And their souls end up less than satisfied.

But GOD is calling you to something better. GOD is calling you to himself. He might be invisible. But he doesn't want to remain hidden. He wants you to seek him, see him, and be completely satisfied with him.

He wants you to venture on a mental pilgrimage until you can smile and say, "GOD is here!"

Beware, Ye Device Lovers!

The practice of seeing and seeking GOD sounds great on paper, but it is challenging in practice.

Because of the robots.

I have a love/hate relationship with the devices in my life. I'm typing on one right now, and when I need a bathroom break, I'll probably take another one with me to the bathroom.* Like you, I love how devices can keep me connected with those I love.

But have you noticed how hard it is to meditate when you are with the machines?

After years of scrolling (the mental equivalent of sitting on the couch and eating Cheetos all week), my brain has gotten flabby. My ability to focus my thoughts on prayer, for example, seems to have rapidly regressed. I chase thought squirrels and wonder how in the world I started with a prayer for our church and ended up in a one-person mental debate about Justin Timberlake's best album.†

---

* Which will probably turn a potty break into a seven-minute scrolling experience.
† Ironically, I just picked up my phone to recall his entire discography and got more than slightly distracted from writing.

When it comes to glorifying GOD, this is a massive issue that deserves careful consideration. To seek GOD means to take your thoughts from here to there, working through the fog until your spiritual eyes see how wonderful he is. This means getting your brain off the digital couch so it has the muscles to meditate and focus.

The Bible puts it this way, "Fix your thoughts on Jesus" (Hebrews 3:1). Fasten your eyes on Jesus. Have a staring contest with the cross. Think about the love that led GOD to send his Son for you, then think about it again, then a third time.

If you are anything like me, this will require some time away from your devices. Although a quick prayer here and a two-minute devotion there can be nice, we rarely see GOD that quickly or easily. Seeking him takes time and mental energy.

But the race is worth it. You might, for the first time in your life, finally see GOD. Once you do, you will love him with all your mind and all your heart.

Ready to move from this abstract idea to the concrete ways you spend your days? It's time to get practical and share my most powerful habit to turn God into GOD.

STUDY QUESTIONS

1. When do you tend to think about GOD? Are there certain times of your day or week when GOD doesn't often cross your mind? If so, why would that be?

2. Name Game Challenge: Text three friends and ask them what they think of when they think of GOD. Compare their answers to the glorious GOD you are starting to read about in this book.

3. Think back on your last church experience. Did you approach that moment with a desire to glorify, worship, and

praise the name of GOD? What might you do differently the next time you are given the chance to gather with other Christians around the Word?

4. Read Psalm 27. Find three connections between a satisfied life and being in GOD's presence.

CHAPTER THREE

"This!"

The Bible is filled with encouragements to seek and see and be satisfied, but what exactly does that look like in daily life? The angels have an advantage—they see how worthy GOD is to be praised and exalted and magnified. But since we can't see what they see, how can we do what they do?

My answer is . . . dogs. And sausage patties. And beer. And buzzer beaters. And avocado toast. And all-inclusive resorts. And sex. And soccer. And flash mobs. And flannel sheets. And grandkids. And good coffee. And everything else that you like about life.

That's what Isaiah taught me.

Around the year 700 BC, a prophet named Isaiah saw the glory of GOD. With his own eyes, in some kind of mysterious vision, he saw what a big deal GOD is. Read Isaiah 6 and you'll find the details of his unforgettable experience, including seeing Jesus exalted on a throne with angels flying all around.

I won't tell you the whole story, but I will let you eavesdrop on the angels. As they flew around Jesus' throne, they sang, "Holy, holy, holy is the LORD Almighty; the whole earth is full of his glory" (v. 3).

Our previous definitions of "holy" and "glory" help us understand their message. Using our modern words, the angels' chorus means, "GOD is wonderfully different! Wonderfully different! Wonderfully different!" And their closing line means, "The whole earth is telling us that GOD is a big deal!"

But please, for the sake of GOD's name, don't miss the location in their lyrics. Where do we find the glory of GOD? Where do we see the proof that GOD is wonderfully different?

"The whole earth."

Not just every square foot of heaven, but every cubic inch of earth is full of GOD's glory.

In other words, if you want to know how big of a deal GOD is, just look around. If you are struggling to think very much of GOD, start by staring at the world around you.

The apostle Paul says something similar when he writes, "God's invisible qualities—his eternal power and divine nature—have been clearly seen, being understood from what has been made" (Romans 1:20).

Though we can't see GOD, we can still experience what GOD is like. We can know a fraction of his love, beauty, friendship, power, joy, delight, wisdom, comfort, and so much more simply by remembering that everything good in this life is a glimpse of GOD.

I call that concept "This!"

"This!" is my one-word summary for saying, "*This* thing is kind of like GOD. GOD created *this* and gave me *this* so I could think more of him. GOD is like *this*, but much better. The way *this* makes me feel is a glimpse of how I will feel when I see his face."

Put into an equation—GOD > "This!"

Put into a logical conclusion—If GOD is better than anything on earth, then GOD must be even better than "This!"

Put into Spanish—DIOS es mejor que esto (aun una carne asada).*

Come to my office and you'll see a decorative wooden block that a member of our church family made for me. It is designed with a single word—"This!" Step into my kitchen and you'll find a piece of art next to the coffeepot that declares, "This!" Walk

---

* If you've ever enjoyed an authentic carne asada, this might be hard to believe.

down my hallway to the closet chalkboard door and you'll see, listed as one of our six family values, "This!"

If you haven't noticed yet, "This!" is a huge deal to my faith. "This!" is how I mentally turn God into GOD. "This!" is how I earnestly seek GOD until I see him. "This!" is the most frequent way I hallow his name. "This!" is how I best keep the commandment to use his name throughout my day, to think more of GOD than ever before.

In a (literally) universal effort to help us think much of GOD, our Creator made everything we see. He created all of "This!" and then created you with the ability to enjoy "This!" He gave you eyes to see beauty, ears to hear melody, taste buds to soak in the savory, and skin to feel the warmth of a friend's hug. He wired your brain with dopamine to feel pleasure and oxytocin to feel affection. GOD made all of "This!" and all of you so that all of life could help you think more of GOD.

In other words, whatever sparks a positive reaction in you is an example of "This!" That reaction might be joy, affirmation, acceptance, relaxation, relief, interest, excitement, curiosity, comfort, laughter, or a deep sense of being loved. But, no matter how incredible the emotion, it is less than 1 percent of the happiness you will experience on the day you see GOD's face.

The Power of "This!"

Think of "This!" like a little trampoline that can launch your heart up to heaven and connect you with GOD. With a little intentionality, you can think more often of GOD throughout your day (quantity) and also think more of GOD himself (quality).

Or you can just keep your head down and stare at your phone, but that would be satisfaction suicide.

Since "This!" is my number one way to turn god/God into GOD, I want to give you an absurd number of examples to explain how it works, broken down into the various categories and scenarios we find ourselves in every day. My hope is that GOD will open your eyes to see how many opportunities you already have to think more of GOD.

My prayer is that before my run-on list is finished, you'll complain, "Okay, Mike, I get it already!" Because once you get "This!", you can get more GOD.

Y'all ready for "This!"?* Here goes:

Friends

- You scan the lunchroom of your new school with a PB&J in hand and rising anxiety in your heart. But then a classmate waves and invites you over to join him and his friends. This is a glimpse of the GOD who invites us to sit with him every day and deepen our relationship through his Word.

- You wonder if you'll be the only student left without a science partner (again) until the girl you like turns around and chooses you. This is a glimpse of the GOD who chose us to be his own before the creation of the world, a choice that we didn't deserve but gladly celebrate.

---

*Recognize the opening line of the classic '90s pre-game song? Listening to jock jams is definitely a "This!" moment. (From 2 Unlimited, "Get Ready for This," on *Get Ready*, Radikal Records, 1992, compact disc.)

- Your best friend knows everything about you—the depression, the abuse you endured, the embarrassing insecurities—yet in love, protects your reputation. This is a glimpse of the GOD whose love always protects us from thoughts of our own unworthiness.
- You take a friend for granted, going months without any effort to invest in your friendship. Yet after your sincere confession, she is willing not only to take you back but also to treat you like your neglect never even happened. This is a glimpse of the GOD who does not treat us as our sins deserve.
- You are going through a divorce and few people are willing to walk with you down that agonizing and lonesome road. Except her. She makes time for you at the times when you need her the most. This is a glimpse of the GOD who walks with us through the darkest valleys and loneliest seasons of life.
- Your work is wearing you down and ruining your day, but then your phone blows up with a texting thread of immature jokes, hilarious selfies, and a smattering of *Dumb and Dumber* quotes. This is a glimpse of GOD, whose words can transform a miserable day and help you forget what you were so upset about.

Are you getting the hang of it? All the relief, excitement, safety, laughter, comfort, and joy are just glimpses of GOD. The whole earth, friends included, are full of his glory!

My friend Shane is an awesome example of "This!" Since he is my accountability partner, I check in with Shane every Sunday night, sharing some key metrics from my week—How much do I weigh? How many hours am I sleeping? How generous am I being with GOD's money? How many alcoholic drinks did I drink? How pure was I in my internet search history? How selfless was I in my marriage? Am I seeking to live at peace with those around me? Et cetera.

The other day, Shane said to me, "I don't care if you fall on your face and fail every day, I want you to tell me the truth. I won't love you any less."

"This!"

This is a glimpse of the faithfulness of GOD. This is a taste of how crazy committed GOD is to his friendship with me. This is what it is like to know that no matter how ugly the struggle, there is a beautiful promise of forgiveness in Jesus.

Family

- Your mom patiently listens and gives you her full attention as you pour out your teenage, twentysomething, or thirty-something problems. This is a glimpse of the GOD who is full of compassion and cares about everything you are going through.

I snorted with laughter when I discovered this picture on my phone. That joy was my "This!"

- Your dad offers some advice about a stressful situation you are facing in life, and his words are filled with the wisdom that only age can provide. This is a glimpse of the GOD whose eternal nature gives him wisdom to guide you through every anxiety-inducing problem.

- Your older brother has your back when someone mocks your acne, haircut, and not-so-straight teeth. This is a glimpse of the GOD who will defend you from every accusation and stand by your side on judgment day.

- Your husband-to-be can't fight back the tears as he watches you walk up the aisle. This is a glimpse of the GOD who rejoices over you as a groom rejoices over his bride (Isaiah 62:5).

- You have finally learned what makes sex good—intimacy, experience, selflessness, and connection—and you're consumed by the passion, pleasure, and closeness you feel after a night with your spouse. This is a glimpse of GOD, whose presence will one day make even the best sex seem boring by comparison.

- You hold your newborn daughter in your arms, wondering how it is possible to love someone so much. This is a glimpse of the GOD who loves you a billion times more than you love your child.

- Your kids are finally home from college, and the board games keep you up late into the evening. This is a glimpse of the GOD whose company will fill your heart and make you hope your time together never ends. Thankfully, it won't.

- You have not always been faithful to your vows to love and respect your spouse. Yet she still comes home to you, night after night. This is a glimpse of the GOD whose faithfulness is great and whose mercy is new every morning.

- You look in the mirror one day and realize you might not ever turn another head again. Yet, despite your wrinkles,

One of my favorite people, my eldest daughter, with one of my favorite creations—a fresh doughnut. Double "This!"

drooping skin, and gray hairs, your husband says you're beautiful. This is a glimpse of the GOD who speaks to us sinners as though we were perfect in his sight.

Do you see the power of "This!"? All that compassion and love are just appetizers to prepare you for the main course of seeing your Father's face.

My mom is a stunning example of "This!" Despite the fact that I am the stereotypical son who does not call as often as he should or talk as long as his mother deserves, my mom loves me. She prays for me. She thinks about me when I'm sick. In eighty-six different ways, she is like Jesus. She babysits my daughters every Friday night so my wife and I can do date night, volunteers to clean my house every week, and then insists that she pay me every month for her part of the cell phone bill (despite refusing to accept payment for the babysitting or cleaning!). *

She is my "This!" This is a flesh-and-blood example of GOD's compassionate heart. This is a glimpse of how much GOD cares for his kids. This is a taste of how absurdly generous GOD is with his sons and daughters.

Nature

- You spend a lazy afternoon exploring a state park. The grass is green. The birds are flirting. The temperature is just right. Your body instinctively takes a deep breath and releases some of your pent-up stress. This is a glimpse of the GOD whose very presence will let you relax in his perfect love.

- Your flower beds burst with life as deep purple tulips emerge from the soil. This is a glimpse of the GOD who delights us when he transforms this broken world into something indescribably beautiful.

- You spend a crisp November afternoon in your tree stand with your phone on Do Not Disturb, uninterrupted by the constant noise of your constantly connected office. This is a glimpse of the GOD who provides peace and rest for our souls.

- You crack your bedroom window during an August shower and smell the fresh rain and let the sounds of summer put you to sleep. This is a glimpse of the GOD whose refreshing power is experienced with every passing storm.

---

* I told you she was like Jesus. And don't be jealous. And no, she is not looking to adopt you.

- You take your first family trip to Florida and stand in front of the Atlantic, staring at the immensity of the ocean. This is a glimpse of the GOD whose love is as deep as the ocean and whose glory is too immense for our minds to grasp.
- You drive through the Rockies for the very first time, humbled by your smallness and captivated by their majesty. This is a glimpse of the GOD whose faithfulness is so great it makes mountains look like speed bumps.
- You head out on an afternoon run and find a deer standing in the middle of the trail. You track him as he gracefully bounds through the woods until he rejoins his family in a small clearing.* This is a glimpse of the GOD who is surprisingly present even when you think you are running through life alone.
- You meet a friend for dinner and tell him the story of chasing a deer during your afternoon run. He shows you a few videos of how deer violently attack people in those very situations.† This is a glimpse of the GOD who has mercy on us and saves us from our foolish decisions.

One of my favorite "This!" moments happened when I jumped out of a plane.

For a guy who is terrified of heights, this wasn't my best idea. And I'm pretty sure I broke the commandment to honor my parents, because my mom was furiously scared she would be left with only my older (and much more handsome and funny and intelligent) brother, Chris.‡ But I jumped anyway.

And I experienced "This!"

---

* This actually happened to me last night! I spent two minutes running after this deer until I met his beautiful family.

† This also happened last night when my friend Shane showed me the video called "Deer Attacks Fat Guy." Yikes!

‡ Chris said he would buy me a Shamrock Shake if I included that parenthetical remark. Mint + ice cream = "This!"

The sun was setting in the west, a full moon rising in the east. The roar of the free fall transformed into the most serene silence as my instructor pulled the rip cord and released the parachute. We floated above GOD's green earth and gaped at what the birds see every day.

But, despite the glory of the moment, it was only momentary.

Thankfully, GOD's glory is more exhilarating and eternally longer lasting than "This!"

Animals

- Your yellow lab nearly breaks off his tail with excitement when you walk through the door, a sight that makes you forget your sour mood from the day. This is a glimpse of the GOD who can inject instant happiness into our hearts with his glorious presence.

- You get into a stupid fight with your girlfriend, but your cat still jumps up on the couch and purrs with delight just to be near you. This is a glimpse of the GOD whose faithfulness never fails, even when we do.

- You take the kids to the zoo and watch their little faces light up as they catch their first closeup looks at lions and tigers and giraffes. This is a glimpse of the GOD whose presence will not only captivate your soul forever, but will delight your loved ones who see him face-to-face.*

- You take a trip to the pet store, spending an hour watching the clown fish, the riveting chameleons, and the irresistibly cute baby pugs. This is a glimpse of the GOD whose beauty will leave us jaw-dropped for all eternity.

- Your yippy (but adorable) dog wakes up the whole house at one in the morning, warning her family that someone is trying to get in the garage door. This is a glimpse of the

---

* Besides seeing the face of GOD for myself, I cannot wait to watch my kids' faces in heaven as they see GOD's face.

GOD whose calls to repent might rattle us but protect us from being robbed of our salvation.

- You lose track of time watching a series of hilarious YouTube videos about "puppy fails." This is a glimpse of the GOD whose wit and timing will make the funniest people here on earth sound like an unprepared introvert on open-mike night.
- You delete your search history before your family finds out you spent an hour watching YouTube videos of puppies. This is a glimpse of the GOD who erases all of our sins to save us from eternal embarrassment on judgment day.

I held a sloth one time. On a family vacation, our cruise ship stopped in Honduras and visited Daniel Johnson's Monkey and Sloth Hangout.* And, true to the name, Dan's team let us hang out with some sloths. We held them like fuzzy backpacks and giggled as we snapped picture after picture.

My youngest daughter, who has not yet hit bottom in her sloth addiction and asked for inpatient help, experienced a bit of GOD that day. When Ben Roethlisberger (or whichever

Hugging Jesus in even better than hugging a sloth!

---

* Where, oddly, all of the animals were named after Pittsburgh Steelers players and pop culture celebrities.

player Dan named him after) turned his slothy head at snail speed and looked her in the eyes with that sloth perma-smile, I expected Jesus to zip her immediately to heaven.

This is a glimpse of GOD. We will be so enamored with GOD's presence that we will wish the moment would never end.

Thankfully, one day, it won't.

Work

- You get an email from a respected client praising you for your above-and-beyond efforts on the new campaign. This is a glimpse of the GOD who cannot wait to recognize you for the good and humble work you have done.
- You're in the zone as ideas come spilling out of your mind at a leadership retreat, energizing your team and reminding you of your GOD-given gifts. This is a glimpse of the GOD whose divine thoughts energize his people and give them lasting hope.
- You bust your tail to meet a crucial deadline, and a co-worker notices your extra efforts, even when your boss doesn't. This is a glimpse of the GOD who notices even the smallest things, even when nobody else says a word.
- You patiently invest eleven hours in a two-year-old whose emotions make the Tower of Terror seem stable, but you somehow sense the divine value of your exhaustion. This is a glimpse of the GOD who promises that nothing we do in his name is ever in vain.
- You read a recent report about unemployment and realize how blessed you are simply to have food on the table. This is a glimpse of the GOD whose undeserved gifts move us to heartfelt worship.

I keep an email file on my work computer called "Encouragement." Every time a thoughtful, kind, or complimentary email arrives, I read it and store it away for a discouraging future day. It never fails to shock me how full that file is despite how flawed I am. Despite my sins and weaknesses, which have let so many people down, GOD has spoken so much life into my heart through those thoughtful messages.

Are you still with me? We are in the homestretch with only a few more trampolines to describe. Plus, we're about to talk about bacon, so you don't want to start skimming now!

Food and Drink

- You smell bacon cooking in the kitchen and hurry to breakfast like Scooby-Doo chasing the scent of his next

Did my kids forget the comma, or should I be worried?

meal. This is a glimpse of the GOD who will overwhelm our senses when we see him in heaven.

- You hold a hot cup of dark roast coffee that warms your body and wakes up your mind. This is a glimpse of the GOD whose presence will shake off every sleepy thought and wake up our souls to worship him for all eternity.
- You take your first bite of Mom's famous lasagna* and immediately have to praise the chef. This is a glimpse of the GOD whose glory will immediately move you to praise him for his creation of the world and his salvation of your soul.
- You try the new Thai restaurant in town, which is so good that you have to rave about it. This is a glimpse of the GOD whose kingdom is so wonderful even angels shout to each other and magnify his glory.
- You take a six-pack of Reese's Peanut Butter Cups out of the freezer and savor the divine mixture of chocolate and peanut butter. This is a glimpse of the GOD whose divine presence will be (believe it or not) even better than that.
- You pick up six gourmet glazed donuts from the local bakery (and eat two before you get home). This is a glimpse of the GOD whose presence is so amazing that we can't wait to get to heaven before we enjoy it.
- You polish off the last bite of decadent chocolate cake and moan, "That was so good." This is a glimpse of the GOD whose goodness will immediately inspire reactions of public praise.
- You finally have a night when your entire family is home to prepare, enjoy, and savor a meal together. This is a glimpse of the GOD who will gather all of his family at an eternal celebration that we will savor together.
- You take time to engage your senses at a Mexican restaurant. The smell of freshly cut cilantro. The crunch of a

---

* My mom makes the best lasagna. Plus, she makes enough for sixteen people even though only six are coming to dinner. And no, she is still not looking to adopt you.

I'm not sure how Moses fully experienced the glory of God without eating sausage. Delicious "This!"

thinly sliced jalapeño. The zing of a citrusy salsa. This is a glimpse of the GOD whose presence is so good we will slow down and enjoy it forever.

• You eat a sausage breakfast sandwich.*

I like scotch.† Not too much of it, since drunkenness robs me of feeling "This!" the next day, but a bit of it is amazing. But you have to drink scotch the right way. After watching a helpful You-Tube tutorial, I learned how to savor scotch, how to maximize the flavors with a triple sniff and a lengthy preswallow swirl around my taste buds. I even mastered the weird sucking-air-in-while-the-scotch-is-still-in-your-mouth thing.

"This!" The flavors surprise me as their intensity grows with a few deep breaths in through the nose. If some fifteen-year-old liquid can delight me like this, what will happen when I breathe in the brilliance of the eternal GOD?

---

* I figured the connection between GOD and sausage would need no further explanation by this point.

† Bonus points if you read that line in your best Ron Burgundy voice.

Six categories down, one to go. Here's the final installment of our study of "This!"

Entertainment

- You squeeze into the stands with tens of thousands of like-minded fans, ready to cheer for your favorite team. This is a glimpse of the GOD who will one day gather Christians from every tribe, race, language, and people to sing his praises together forever.
- You watch a predictable rom-com on a date with your new girlfriend in which, despite a few relational hiccups, two people live happily ever after. This is a glimpse of the GOD who, despite our sins against him, promises to forgive us so we can live happily ever after with him.*
- You switch stations and stumble across your favorite song from your teenage years.† You crank the volume and sing loud enough for people in nearby cars to hear. This is a glimpse of the GOD whose greatness will call you to sing no matter how many people are within earshot.
- Your buddy sends you a clip from *Tommy Boy* that you click open during a brutally long staff meeting. This is a glimpse of the GOD who brings joy and relief during the tedious stretches of life on earth.
- Your co-workers cover their faces when your *Tommy Boy* clip plays at full volume, revealing your relative immaturity for a business professional. This is a glimpse of the GOD who will make sure that you are not ashamed on the day when all of our secrets are revealed.

---

* Watching these movies should be my wife's most frequent "This!", reminding her of the sacrifices that Jesus and I make to prove our love for her.

† Which, of course, should be "Hey Ya!" by OutKast. Or some late-'90s hip-hop. Am I dating myself with these examples?

World Cup 2010. The basement television set. My face nearly glued to the screen. Injury time against Algeria. US midfielder Landon Donovan races up the field as the seconds tick away. (Describing the moment a decade later still makes my heart race.) A cross into the box. A flick that the goalie deflects. And then Landon—sweet Landon!—comes racing in to smash the ball into the empty net. I race up the stairs in a delusional frenzy and run around my neighborhood screaming myself hoarse.

"This!!!"

This is a glimpse of the final victory of GOD, when Jesus returns on the last day and his people party for all eternity.

Whew! "This!"

The apostle Paul once told the Christians at Corinth, "So whether you eat or drink or whatever you do, do it all for the glory of God" (1 Corinthians 10:31). With every bite, every sip, every whatever, we acknowledge GOD's glory. We do it remembering and declaring that GOD is a big deal.

Life is like a trampoline park. On every side of your life there are spring-loaded "This!" moments with the potential to launch your thoughts up to GOD. You can stick to the springless dividers in between them and set your mind on earthly things. Or you can bounce on every earthly blessing and lift your heart up to the Holy One.

So here's the challenge: Glorify GOD in a thousand little ways today. Practice godly mindfulness and learn to see his glory in the flowers and friendships and laughter. Because GOD did not create the world for a mere Instagram photo and a few dozen likes.

In fact, pause and think of the last twenty-four hours. What good things did you experience? What rest or joy or pleasure did GOD provide you? And what was he trying to teach you about himself in the process?

I'm not sure about your list, but I know the answer to that final question. He created it all so that you could know him, love him, and think much of him.

Sister Earth

You may have noticed how so many of the previous examples were rooted in nature—the sights and sounds of life here on earth. The more I seek GOD and see his glory on our planet, the more I find myself thinking about environmental issues.

Like me, you might not be the biggest tree hugger on your block. I have never chained myself to a sapling at a construction site. You personally might care more about convenience than conservation.

But can I plant one seed in the soil of your brain? Every time a piece of GOD's creation gets destroyed, GOD gets harder to see. Every time a species goes extinct, there is one less opportunity for the next round of humans to stand in awe of GOD.

If "the heavens declare the glory of God" (Psalm 19:1), what happens when smog makes the heavens hard to see?

If GOD's nature and power "have been clearly seen, being understood from what has been made" (Romans 1:20), what happens when we no longer see some of the creatures he has made?

There is, of course, a balance here. The earth, like everything else, is in bondage to decay (Romans 8:21), and no recycling push or conservation plan can totally prevent it.

However, if earth endures for another one hundred years or ten thousand years, I want my great-grandchildren to see the stars, dip their toes in the oceans, and hold the sloths, so they can see GOD as I do.

So, as you make decisions that impact our earth, let's help the next generation think much of GOD.

You Are Their "This!"

A few years back, I read a leadership book that encouraged me to craft a personal mission statement—a short and sweet, memorable line that would hang on the wall and remind me of the reason I exist.

No pressure, right?

This was before my Psalm 73 epiphany, so I didn't think much about GOD's glory and presence in those days. However, GOD must have been nudging me in that direction, because what I chose was essentially a wordy way to say, "This!"

My mission statement read, "My mission is to reflect the character of God in everything I do."

I went on to explain how I wanted my children to know the love of our heavenly Father through my love as their earthly father. I wanted my wife to grasp the goodness of being part of the bride of Christ by the way I treated and cherished her. I wanted my church to know what it was like to have Jesus as their Good Shepherd by the way I guided, nourished, and protected them with the Word of GOD.

In other words, my mission was to be their "This!" I wanted the people in my life to see a glimpse of GOD when they saw me.

And that is your mission too.

You might be organized or spontaneous, thoughtful or humorous. You might know how to lighten the mood, connect with someone who is socially awkward, or cast an inspiring vision for the future. Maybe you have a high-powered job or feel like another cog in the company machine. You may be the captain of the varsity squad or the backup to the backup punter. You might be a respected volunteer at your church or a member who flies under the radar. You might write books, change diapers, prepare publicity campaigns, or unclog toilets. Christians have radically different roles in life, but no matter what you do or what gifts you have, your mission is to be "This!" to others.

Jesus said it this way, "Let your light shine before others, that they may see your good deeds and glorify your Father in heaven" (Matthew 5:16). People glorify GOD, they remember what a big deal he is, when they see your goodness, patience, forgiveness, compassion, selflessness, and generosity.

So, when you take time to write an encouraging email, the recipient can say, "This is how encouraged I will feel in the presence of GOD."

And when you put down your phone and give your son your full attention, your son can think, "This is how much GOD pays attention to me."

And when you surprise the bored cashier with genuine conversation, she can think, "This is how much time GOD has for me."

And when you unload the dishwasher even though it's officially your wife's chore, she can think, "This is how much GOD serves me."

And when you have hard conversations that lead to actual reconciliation, your friend can think, "This is how much GOD wants to keep being close to me."

You Are Their "This!"

Think of yourself like the moon. It lights up the sky and inspires poets and songwriters. But the only reason you see the moon is because of the sun. The moon is only reflecting the light that comes from an unseen source. Just like you reflect the light of the unseen GOD.

Don't you love the purpose and potential of that idea? You exist to help people think the most important thought in the world—GOD!

Every moment of every day, you can be their "This!"

STUDY QUESTIONS

1. Explain the concept of "This!" in your own words.

2. Think back on the past twenty-four hours. Where was GOD revealing his glory to you? Did you notice "This!" in the moment?

3. Out of my long list of "This!" examples, which three opened your eyes to the glory of GOD in your own life?

4. How could you "be their 'This!'" in the next week?

CHAPTER FOUR

Two Unexpected Ways to Meet GOD

The more I realize how hard it is to think much of GOD, the more I understand why Jesus organized religion.

Seriously.

Now, if you are like most people, you have some issues with organized religion. And rightfully so. Today, more than ever in history, we see and hear and read about the sins of those within the church: the shameless greed, sexual improprieties, tragic abuse, man-made rules, blatant hypocrisy, and lack of love. Put all the headlines together, and organized religion seems like something to be avoided, not applauded.

I get why so many people want to be independently spiritual and not religiously organized. Yet Jesus, who himself experienced the ugliness of church gone wrong, nevertheless wanted us all to live in community, to gather around the Word regularly, and to put ourselves under loving spiritual authority.

Why? Because we don't think much of GOD. Our hearts default to thinking little of GOD, believing he might be nice but he's not the only thing we need. Throughout the week, our minds are excited about a potential promotion, a big game, or the start of hunting season, but not that excited about GOD. Which, as we have seen, is a death sentence for our souls.

But then we go to church. And (hopefully!) the service helps us think about GOD. We sing songs about the miraculous things he has done. We remember that GOD is the Creator of all things. We confess that GOD is the Savior of sinners, bursting with mercy and compassion. We pray for GOD's name to be wonderful and for him to get all the glory, for the entire world to believe that GOD is a big deal.

And the people sitting around us are the proof that we need GOD. Successful business people are there, silently teaching us that six-figure salaries cannot satisfy the soul. Popular people are there, reminding us of popularity's inability to quench the deepest thirsts of our hearts. Beautiful and powerful and married people are there, proving that looks and leverage and love are good, but they are not great enough to fill the GOD-shaped hole in our hearts.

We need these people so we don't believe the lie that more of _____ will make us eternally happy.

These people, fellow Christians whom you have come to know and value, the ones you've prayed for and with, the ones whose confessions you have heard and whose ears have heard yours, the ones whose bills you have helped pay and whose dinner tables you have broken bread at, these people see you and smile. They are your regular "This!", a glimpse of the faithfulness of GOD, who knows so much about you yet refuses to walk away.

Then the Scripture is read. And, unlike 99.9 percent of what we read on social media feeds, this is about GOD. For the first time all week, instead of staring in a mirror and thinking of yourself, your thoughts fixate on GOD. His kindness. His patience. His power.

Then the pastor preaches. He doesn't "give a talk" or "share some thoughts" as if he were a gifted employee with a knack for public speaking. He preaches as one called and sent by GOD himself with a word for GOD's people, speaking with authority about the glory of GOD and GOD's love for humankind.

The pastor is unafraid to call you out, to warn you about loving your reputation or your sense of control or anything more than GOD. He warns you with sad stories of people who pursued the temporary things of this world and left GOD in the rearview mirror. In love, he refuses to let you walk the path of short-term pleasure that dead-ends in long-term pain.*

And because he is compelled to share the glorious grace of GOD, he points you to the cross of Jesus, where unconditional love was on shocking display. He connects the dots, explaining how Jesus points you to GOD, the only true refuge and rock in this uncertain world.

And, long after the service is over, the pastor prays for you. In the quiet of his office, as he slowly works his way through the names of his church family, he prays for you. He asks GOD to protect you from the lies that lead to disappointment. He begs the Holy Spirit to open your eyes to see how wonderful GOD truly is.

This is why Jesus organized the religion that would carry on his teaching. While he wouldn't endorse every man-made rule or custom from the past two millennia, Jesus did want a consistent, regular way for you to connect with the Word of GOD and the people of GOD, which both remind you of the glory of GOD.

Is it messy? For sure. Are all the people, the pastor included, severely flawed? No doubt. Will GOD use those flaws to expose the conditionality of your love and, by contrast, the stunning unconditionality of his? Absolutely. Even the church's flaws are a way to think more of GOD.

Recently, I experienced that very thing. Our church family gathered for another Sunday service, and GOD was on display that day. Jonathan, our worship leader, led us in the song "Hosanna." My voice joined the hundreds around me in the opening lines,

* Kudos to Pastor Ski, the founding pastor of The CORE, for the memorable saying "STP = LTP."

70

which reminded us all of the power of GOD's presence to erase our fears and fill us with hope.

Our hearts are stirring and yearning and longing for GOD. Why? Because simply being with him gives us strength. His very presence washes away our fears for the day. These words led me to worship, to seek GOD until I could see GOD.

Then Pastor Michael* took the stage. He read Psalm 13 to us, an ancient song that cries out to GOD in the midst of stubborn and persistent pain. But the Psalm ended with these words: "But I trust in your unfailing love; my heart rejoices in your salvation. I will sing the LORD's praise, for he has been good to me" (vv. 5–6).

Why do we have joy, even when our pain covers and clings to us like flakes on a dry scalp? Why would we praise GOD on days when we reach for another Advil? Because we trust in his unfailing love. Though our bodies and friends and families fail, GOD's love never does. That reading prompted a quiet "Amen" from the congregation.

Then Pastor Tim got up to preach on Psalm 73, the very psalm that launched me on this spiritual journey. I scribbled notes and smiled as I thought more and more about GOD, then joined the author in declaring, "But as for me, it is good to be near God" (v. 28). If he was some unimpressive god, being near him wouldn't be that good. But since a week of "This!" moments had taught me otherwise, that verse stirred my soul. I am near GOD! By grace, GOD is here!

After the service, a guest asked me about our small-group Bible studies, and I told the story of how I found true community at our church, people who knew me better than anyone on the planet does yet loved me persistently—a glimpse of GOD's no-strings-attached love. Then I ducked into my office, where every single book on every single shelf had been wrapped like a Christmas gift, an elaborate prank from some amazing friends who invested

---

* This is not me, but the other pastor at our church. Just because we like to keep our guests totally confused.

over twenty hours of labor in the surprise! I thought about how much I am loved despite my obvious flaws. And that thought made me think of the friendship I have with the GOD of love.

And all of this happened in under ninety minutes.

Now, I know that not every Sunday is that good. Sometimes you go to church and hear a confusing message or a less-than-passionate song of praise. But GOD knows that a regular diet of gathered worship makes you spiritually strong.

So, I encourage you to connect to a community. Find a community organized around the Word of GOD in order to open the eyes of the people of GOD to the surpassing worth of GOD. Because something as life changing as a satisfied heart will not come easily. The devil will not let it. You will need lots of help. And GOD would love to give lots of help, love, and belonging to you through church.

The Power of Pain, aka "That"

But what about those days, or decades, when life seems to be This-less? If today's goal is to think more of GOD, what do you do when life is more painful than pleasurable?

Maybe that thought crossed your mind when reading all the examples of "This!" listed above. Maybe your past week was not filled with faithful friends, delicious food, and loving family. What then?

Let's be real. Sometimes life is not just hard; it is brutal. A car accident or a malignant tumor turns an average year into your worst ever. You find yourself in the pit of depression and can't even motivate yourself to shower. You try to heal your brain from the trauma you suffered as a child or overseas at war but progress is hard to see. You're bullied at school or end up broke without work. How do seasons like these fit into all this talk of joy and peace and satisfaction with GOD?

Though it can be hard to imagine, according to the apostle Paul, pain is one of the most powerful tools to make you think much, much more of GOD.

Here's my go-to passage on this subject, taken from one of the Bible's most raw chapters on suffering, Romans 8: "I consider that our present sufferings are not worth comparing with the glory that will be revealed in us" (v. 18).

Paul has pulled out the balance scale to see which weighs more, our present sufferings or the glory that will be revealed. But before we begin to take down measurements, Paul says our sufferings are so small by comparison to GOD's glory that it's "not worth comparing" them.

That should stun you.

Because Paul did not live a pampered life. He was beaten, imprisoned, stoned, left for dead, abandoned, rejected, slandered, and unappreciated. Homeless, hungry, an object of injustice, Paul tasted suffering. Many of his Christian friends were murdered or tortured. Paul's agony wasn't the increasing cost of cable or spotty Wi-Fi. He spent hard nights in the pit of pain.

So, Paul stacked all that suffering on one side of the scale. Next he heaped up all the pain and grief and frustration of his fellow Christians (notice the "our" in "our present sufferings"?). Just imagine the weight of all those broken hearts as Paul placed them on the scale.

Then, to the opposite end of the scale, Paul added a final weight— the glorious GOD.

He thought of the glory that would be revealed when Jesus returned, transforming our broken bodies and making every spiritual blessing visible. Glancing from side to side, Paul measured all of the church's pain against all of the coming glory.

His final conclusion? It's not even close. He didn't need his glasses to look more closely at the numbers.

Just think of what that must mean. If all the suffering we've endured doesn't even register on the scale compared to GOD, how wondrous must GOD be? If miscarriages and chronic sciatica and marriage betrayals and racial injustice don't tip the scales when weighed next to GOD, how satisfying must GOD be?

Let's be clear. Christianity is not about ignoring pain. Rather, in the pain, it looks to GOD and insists, "You must be so good! Because this hurts so bad."

Then, GOD leverages your pain to draw you, in his own mysterious way, into his presence and love.

Maybe you could remember this idea with a single word: "That."

Just like "This!" can get your heart to GOD, "That" can too. Every time life is not funny or fascinating, you can still trampoline your thoughts up to the GOD who is here. You can say:

"That" pain will be nothing next to the pleasure of seeing GOD's face.

I won't even think about "That" when GOD's glory is revealed.

"That" won't happen ever again once I fully experience GOD's love.

GOD has something so good that it will make me forget about all of "That."

"That" is much harder than "This!", but it is a powerful way to think more of GOD.

I love how author Paul Tripp puts it in his book entitled *Suffering*: "Everything in life ends or dies in some way. Nothing in this world remains the same forever. Many of the things we bank on end up failing us in the end. But God never will."[1]

Notice how Paul is imitating the apostle who shares his name? He is not avoiding the wretched realities of life on earth. But he is using them to think more of GOD.

Let Your Pain Preach

74

Tripp reminds us how constant and faithful GOD is, even in the midst of our pain: "Few people suffer from the fact that their God is too large! . . . With his here-forever presence comes his here-forever wisdom, his here-forever grace, his here-forever strength, his here-forever authority, his here-forever love, his here-forever mercy, his here-forever righteousness, and his here-forever patience."[2]

No one wants to suffer in this life. But when suffering comes, please don't waste it. Leverage the hard days to get back to GOD, to exalt his name, and to lean on the One who can provide the joy you need to suffer well.

GOD's Purpose for Your Pain

Author Kathy Keller once told the story of a helpless bird and a seemingly cruel lumberjack to describe GOD's purposes for our pain.[3]

The bird had just built a warm nest high in a tree when the lumberjack showed up at the base of the trunk. Turning his ax-head to the blunt, flat side, he thwapped the tree, sending vibrations up the trunk and through the nest.

Thwapp! Thwapp! Thwapp!

He smacked the tree again and again until the frustrated bird flew away and started to build a new nest in a new tree.

But just when the second nest was built, the lumberjack appeared again, ax in hand and eyes on the bird.

Thwapp! Thwapp! Thwapp!

He swung his ax against the bark, refusing to stop until the bird once again flew away and left her nest. A third time it happened. Then a fourth. Just when the nests were perfectly shaped, the lumberjack showed up, harassing the poor bird who was so desperate to sit down and rest.

Finally, with an angry squawk the frustrated bird flew just past the edge of the forest and started to build her nest in the side of a rocky cliff. Once finished, she sat down, breathed a deep sigh of relief, and snuggled into her new home.

The lumberjack looked up and smiled, and just then he heard the trucks arrive to clear out all the trees in the forest.

Like the lumberjack, GOD knows that sooner or later everything you love will be gone. In this world, stuff never lasts. So, before we build a home for our hearts in some temporary thing, GOD intervenes. He uses the struggles and inconveniences of life to force us to keep searching for something more stable, something where we can actually find peace.

Something like a rock that won't move.

Something like GOD.

One Word Down, Two to Go

So far, we have unpacked and examined the GOD who is the key to our epic sentence—GOD is here! Before we move on to the second word, let's review what we have learned.

Our primary problem is thinking too little of GOD.

Our primary solution is thinking much more of GOD.

We think much of GOD when we hallow and glorify and praise his name.

We accomplish that by directing our focus to "This!", the glimpses of GOD's glory we experience throughout our day.

We can also accomplish that through "That," those painful moments that will one day be eclipsed by GOD's glory.

Without a massive, happiness-inducing, praise-inspiring, peace-giving GOD, the rest of the sentence won't matter. But if you have come to love and long for GOD, then the next word will mean the world to you.

So, before our journey continues, let me pray for you.

My Best Prayer for You

When the apostle Paul prayed for the Christians in Ephesus, he said, "I keep asking that the God of our Lord Jesus Christ, the glorious Father, may give you the Spirit of wisdom and revelation, so that you may know him better" (Ephesians 1:17).

The Ephesians were already Christians, already convinced that Jesus was the only way to be forgiven and saved. They knew the one true GOD and trusted in the good news that enabled them to enjoy GOD's presence. Even still, Paul longed for his friends and fellow Christians to "know [GOD] better." He prayed that the Holy Spirit would use every possible "This!" in creation and all the promises of Jesus' salvation to make the Ephesians think more of GOD.

And that is my prayer for you, that you will remember that GOD is here. I pray that the Holy Spirit would rid your heart of some unimpressive, easily forgotten view of your Father and replace it with the glorious GOD whose presence is better than all we could ever imagine.

I pray that you would actually believe in GOD.

STUDY QUESTIONS

1. How might my case for organized religion encourage a friend or family member to reconnect to church?

2. Explain the concept of "That" in your own words.

3. Paul Tripp writes, "Few people suffer from the fact that their God is too large!" How does this statement support the big idea of this book?

4. Read Ephesians 1:15–23. List four glorious truths about GOD that you discovered in these verses. Join Paul in his prayer that we all might know GOD better.

PART 2

GOD Is _____.

CHAPTER FIVE

Hungry for Eternity

"Grab a leg," the doctor ordered. So I wrapped two nervous hands around my wife's right leg.

My wife was giving birth to our first baby, and the doctor gave me a front-row seat.* Our prayers for a baby, delayed for so many years, were finally being answered. Kim pushed and huffed and pushed again, while I did my best imitation of a deer at a spotlight convention.

And then our baby girl came. Our little Brooklyn.†

Like never before in my life, I sobbed for joy. I have no clue what the weather was that day or how much money we had in our checking account or what percentage of my co-workers liked me at the time because that baby girl captured my heart. Just seeing her made me forget about my problems and struggles. Looking into her face flooded me with emotions that I still remember a decade later.

That, ladies and gentlemen, is the power of presence.

---

* Apparently the days of dads hanging out in the lobby with their buddies and a few cigars are long gone.

† Who was named after the Brooklyn-style pizza advertised on a Domino's box during Kim's pregnancy. True story.

Whether you've watched the birth of a child or not, I bet you know the power of presence. When the right person walks into the room, they have the power to make everything else fade out of focus. Your annoying co-workers or student loans or disappointing love life might not change, but they turn blurry and dim, like stars that disappear when the sun rises in the morning.

That's the power of presence. Few things are as powerful as changing a "was" or a "will be" into the present tense "is."

Recently I conducted an experiment on this very subject. I asked people, "If you could pick any person to walk through that door right now, who would make you the happiest?"

One waitress said, "My boyfriend."

Another person answered, "My dog."

But Katie, a friend who cuts my hair, offered my favorite answer. She said, "I'm supposed to say Jesus, right?" Then, after a millisecond pause, "Because I'd love to see a dolphin! Or maybe a guy bringing sushi! Wait! Could the dolphin be delivering sushi? Because that would make me *so* happy!"

I love Katie's honesty. As a Christian, she knew the right answer, but what got her heart racing was the thought of sushi-delivering dolphins.

Like Katie, we now realize that GOD is glorious enough to give us peace, joy, and satisfaction. If experiencing "This!" can change our days, imagine if I pointed toward the door and shouted, "GOD is here!"

But like Katie, I wonder if we ever replace GOD with some unreliable substitute. We put our hope and our happiness in something or someone that is not guaranteed to be here.

You might be waiting for the affection of a significant other or a *new* significant other, for your father to show up and affirm you or apologize for that one thing he said, for your kids to come home and spend time with you or appreciate you for all you did, for some new customer to hire you or an old one to come crawling back. You might be praying for the presence of a cancer-free PET scan, a hefty tax return, or a sunny forecast for your vacation.

But also like Katie, you might glance at the door and realize that what you hoped for isn't coming. Sometimes the doorknob never turns. Maybe it will one day, but not today.

Why not? Why are so few of our days filled with the presence of the people and stuff we so deeply want? Why is so little of life as satisfying as we crave?

Because the whole world has gone to hevel.

When It All Goes to Hevel

Hevel is a Hebrew word that fills one of the Bible's most intriguing books—Ecclesiastes. It means "mist" or "vapor." Like a puff of air from your lips on a ten-degree day, hevel appears one second and disappears the next. Its existence is so short-term that one translation renders hevel "meaningless."

Right around 1000 BC, King Solomon of Israel decided to dedicate his money, time, and wisdom to conduct an experiment on human happiness. He wrote, "I, the Teacher, was king over Israel in Jerusalem. I applied my mind to study and to explore by wisdom all that is done under the heavens" (Ecclesiastes 1:12–13). Solomon's goal was to try every path, explore every angle, and figure out what was the best way to be happy.

So he did. Solomon used his GOD-given wisdom, his royal resources, and his extended PTO in the pursuit of lasting happiness. And what did he learn? That everything, even the best things, are hevel.

Solomon started with sexual pleasure (Ecclesiastes 2:1). He installed a rotating door in his bedroom, spinning through the supermodels of the ancient Near East. Over one thousand women officially called Solomon their man, meaning the king could have sex with a different girl at breakfast, lunch, and dinner for a year before sleeping with the first woman for the second time.

But the pleasure of all that passion was hevel.

So Solomon switched tracks and tried a more laid-back life—laughter, wine, and nights on the town (Ecclesiastes 2:3). He hired the best harpists in Israel and didn't dare to sip wine from a box.

But the excitement for another party was hevel.

So Solomon decided to grow up a bit, become more business minded, and take on great projects for his community. After that, he explored the rigors of philosophy. Next, he tried leaving a legacy of justice to protect the next generation of those down-and-out. Then he focused on his family and the comfortable life he could leave them when he was gone.

But all of it, every attempt and every angle, was hevel.

Everything Is Hevel

Solomon lamented, "'Meaningless! Meaningless!' says the Teacher. 'Utterly meaningless! Everything is meaningless'" (Ecclesiastes 1:2). In this life, everything is temporary. In this world, nothing "is here" for very long. Everything is only briefly present.

No matter how much you want it, pray for it, or beg GOD to bless it, everything appears in a moment, then disappears in the next. Even family. Even friends. Even health. Even wealth. Everything.

You can always say, "_____ was here," or "_____ might be here one day." But no matter how you fill in the blank, it won't be true for very long.

So, what is the wisest man GOD ever made trying to tell us? That if you want lasting peace, joy, satisfaction, and happiness in this life, it might not be found in the places you assume.

Because everything is meaningless. Before long, everything goes to hevel.

When "This!" Is a Problem

So what are you pursuing to make you happy? What, at the end of the day, do you need in order to feel content with your life? I'm not asking what would be *nice*, but what you *need* to rejoice today?

If your answer is any version of "This!" instead of the GOD every "This!" is pointing to, you have a major problem on your hands. Your joy is as close to disappearing as that puff of breath on a frigid day.

Because, unless Solomon was dead wrong, your happiness is on death row. Something will happen tomorrow or the next day, and—poof!—the thing you need to rejoice will disappear like a mist. Everything is hevel.

And Solomon would hate to see that happen to you. GOD would too.

The issue with everything in this life is that it often "isn't." We can't guarantee it will be present. It either never shows up or it leaves too soon. Which means that if your joy is based on any version of "This!", you are one bad moment away from a joyless life. One ungrateful customer. One unfaithful boyfriend. One concerning symptom. One flat tire. One unnoticed post. One unfair criticism.

No wonder your joy is such an endangered species.

I once gave a presentation on GOD and the dangers of putting our hope in anything else to an auditorium of educators. I brought out my daughter's favorite stuffed animal and set it on stage. "Meet Joy, everyone," I introduced. I explained the most common places where Christians find their joy—their families, ministries, achievements, or personal well-being.

Next, I asked for one of the teachers to come up and represent life, which has a way of making everything maddeningly temporary. A quiet, middle-aged man volunteered to join me up front. "I would like you to destroy Joy," I encouraged him. "You can step on her or kick her or trample her under your feet." He silently nodded in understanding.

But I did not expect what happened next.

85

This mild-mannered teacher unleashed his inner WWE wrestler. He brutalized that poor stuffed animal, smashing it into the stage floor. In classic Hulk Hogan style, he raised a threatening elbow, tapped it twice, and dropped a crushing blow onto Joy before drop-kicking her into the shocked crowd.[*]

That poor stuffy never stood a chance.[†]

My point was abundantly clear, thanks to my rather intense volunteer. If your joy is just wandering through this world, something or someone is bound to drop an elbow on your joy and punt happiness far from your heart.

If we place our joy in something temporary, our joy will be temporary. "This!" is good, but it is never GOD. "This!" will always be a temporary glimpse, vanishing in a moment and lasting far less time than your heart needs to be continually happy.

If your joy lives in a codependent relationship with anything on earth, then your joy is dependent on something undependable. You don't want that. The wisest man in history doesn't want that for you either.

King Solomon warns, "Hopes placed in mortals die with them" (Proverbs 11:7).

"This!" is so nice, but please don't tell yourself you need it, because your hope will die when "This!" disappears.

Why Hevel Can't Make Your Heart Happy

If we know that everything is temporary, why can't we convince our hearts to be happy when something is here instead of frustrated when it isn't?

For example, every one of us knows we cannot please everyone all the time. So when someone expresses an ugly critique about our weight, haircut, intelligence, or performance at work, why do

[*] I guess that's what happens when you spend all week with a bunch of fourth graders!

[†] But luckily, without bones and internal organs, this stuffy fully recovered from the abuse.

we sink into an emotional funk that consumes our car ride home and probably ends in an empty pint of double-chocolate frozen custard on our couch? Why does one critique have such power?

Our brain should know better. Everyone else we encountered either had nothing bad to say or said something good, so why is one word so devastating? Why does today's headache make us forget the thousands of days that were headache-free? Why aren't we more grateful for the years we had with a special someone instead of lamenting the years after his funeral? Why are we so quick to pray, "Fix this one thing!" and so slow to praise, "Thank you for these thousand things!"? Why do we get so used to being blessed that we cannot emotionally handle it when we aren't?

King Solomon can answer that question. "[GOD] has also set eternity in the human heart" (Ecclesiastes 3:11).

GOD put a longing for eternity in your heart. Within your soul is a craving for good things to last. You were made to be discontent with temporary blessings. All those desires in you for love and friendship and purpose will never be satisfied by a little "This!" here and there. No, you were created for much, much more.

The Hunger of Your Heart

I'd bet my best Bible that your heart has said, "Amen!" to Solomon's assertion.

You want to be loved by your boyfriend or girlfriend always, not just on Tuesdays and Thursdays. You want to be encouraged by your classmates and teachers from orientation day until graduation day, not just a year or two of your high school career. You want to be affirmed by your father always, not just until you turn ten. You want to be valued always, not told you are worthless every other week. You want to be treasured always, not told you were a mistake by one of your parents. You want to be safe always, not live in fear of assault eight hours of every day. You want to be blessed always, not cursed for six months every year.

That "always and forever" is part of your heart's DNA. Your Creator put it there, and no matter how religious or spiritual you may or may not be, that hunger and thirst exists. We all share the same desire—to find something really good that really lasts.

In the book of Proverbs, Solomon gave one example of your heart's eternal desires: "What a person desires is unfailing love" (Proverbs 19:22). What your heart really wants is to shout, "Love is here! Love is here! Love is here!" without ever having to cry, "Love was here" or, "Love is over there."

Yet, Solomon also wrote, "Many claim to have unfailing love, but a faithful person who can find?" (Proverbs 20:6).

Our hearts crave an eternal "is." They will never be satisfied with a "was" or a "will be." They want—no, they need!—something that is right here, right now. Which describes only one person in the entire universe: GOD.

That eternal longing can only be satisfied when we seek the face of GOD, where love and acceptance and approval last forever.

But when we ignore Solomon's advice and try to fill our hearts with a temporary something instead of an eternal Someone, our satisfaction sputters like a 1993 Geo Tracker with faulty wiring.

A.W. Tozer wrote about this decades before the inventions of video games and smartphones: "Your poor heart, in which God put appreciation for everlastingness, will not take electronic gadgets in lieu of eternal life."[1]

Saint Augustine, a famous Christian from the fourth century, echoes Tozer's point in a famous prayer: "You have made us with yourself as our goal, and our heart is restless until it rests in you."[2]

Until you rest in the truth that GOD is here, your heart will be restless.

Six Guys and Why You Are Thirsty for GOD[*]

The prophet Jeremiah and our Savior, Jesus, talked about this eternal hole in your heart as a spiritual thirst. The metaphor is powerful, because when you are thirsty, nothing else matters. You can be rocking Gucci slippers, but if you're dying of thirst, you are not a happy camper.[†]

Back around 600 BC, Jeremiah wept as he watched his neighbors worship gods that could not quench the thirst in their hearts. For decades, he passionately reached out his arms and raised up his voice, begging them to come back to the only One who could satisfy their longings.

Quoting GOD, Jeremiah preached, "My people have committed two sins: They have forsaken me, the spring of living water, and have dug their own cisterns, broken cisterns that cannot hold water" (Jeremiah 2:13).

Instead of seeking his face, GOD's people abandoned him, the spring of living water.

Think about that. A spring continually brings fresh water from down in the water table up to the earth's surface so we can drink and live. In a similar way, GOD doesn't make you work or dig down deep to find his love. Instead, he brings it bubbling up into

---

[*] I am well aware of the modern use of the word "thirsty" (slang for "sexually desperate"), but I trust you'll understand that this section has little to do with sex. Most of the sex talk was back in the "This!" section.

[†] And you are also pretty clueless for packing Gucci slippers and no water for your camping trip.

your life. Better yet, he invites you to "drink" as much of that love as you want without cost (Isaiah 55:1).

But, "They have forsaken me," GOD groaned. They left behind the gushing spring of GOD's grace to dig their own cisterns, to find an alternative source to quench their thirst.

An underground reservoir for storing rainwater, a good cistern would collect rain and provide people with plenty of clean water to drink. Except these man-made cisterns were "broken cisterns that cannot hold water." The rain fell in . . . then leaked out the bottom. Leaving the people thirsty. Dehydrated. Dying.

Which is what their gods did too. GOD substitutes promised much but delivered little. And people ended up with parched souls and spiritual cotton mouth.

The Jews of Jeremiah's day were relatively religious people. They prayed. They believed in something more than themselves. They even gathered for worship here and there. But they did not seek GOD with their whole hearts. They didn't see him as the satisfying solution to their cravings. They looked elsewhere for that.

The same thing can happen to you. You can be a believer and still dig your own cisterns in an attempt to find happiness apart from the presence of GOD. When the first raindrops of romance or athletic success or living for the weekend fall, you will assume that you are living the good life. But those cisterns are cracked.

Spring or Cistern?

And sooner or later, they will all be empty. You'll age out of the honeymoon stage and question if they're really the one. You'll go to college where no one cares about your high school rushing yards or relative popularity. You'll start with the buzz and end up with the crushing needs of an alcoholic. Your soul will dry out.

And you'll wish you had a spring to drink from.

Thankfully, Jesus says you do.

Six hundred years after Jeremiah preached, Jesus sat down by a well and waited for the thirsty woman who had worn out her wedding gown digging a broken cistern called romance. She came that day with a water jar and a thirst, not just for a cool drink from the town well, but for something to quench the eternal thirst in her soul. Jesus' initial small talk surprised her (a Jewish man talking to a non-Jewish woman?!), but then things got deeper.

"Everyone who drinks this water will be thirsty again," Jesus declared, "but whoever drinks the water I give them will never thirst. Indeed, the water I give them will become in them a spring of water welling up to eternal life" (John 4:13–14).

Sound familiar?

This woman knew how much work it was to walk to the well, lower her bucket, and strain her shoulders to lug the water back up. And how frustrating it was to do the same work day after day as her thirst returned. Which is why Jesus' offer intrigued her. Never thirst again? A spring instead of a well? Water that comes up to me instead of me going down to it? She wanted in.

But Jesus wanted to save her from more than sore muscles. He wanted to deal with her unsatisfied soul.

"Go, call your husband and come back," Jesus ordered, in what must have seemed like a tangent at best and a rude assumption at worst (v. 16). But Jesus knew exactly what he was saying. He knew that, like Jeremiah's cracked cisterns, the men in her past couldn't quench her heart's thirst.

"'I have no husband,' she replied. Jesus said to her, 'You are right when you say you have no husband. The fact is, you have had five husbands, and the man you now have is not your husband'" (John 4:17–18).

Ouch. Five husbands. Enough wedding rings to fill a whole hand. And a promise ring on the other hand. This woman needed GOD—the only trustworthy source of constant, unconditional love. She was wasting her life worshiping men, which is why Jesus didn't give her ten tips on making marriage work but one massive revelation: "I, the one speaking to you—I am he" (v. 26).

I am he. Jesus was saying, "I am the Messiah. I am the one who will get you to GOD. I am the giver of living water. I am an unfailing spring. I gush with the gift of eternal life. I am offering you unending access to a thirst-quenching GOD."

Do you know what she did? She left her jar behind (v. 28). That symbol of her never-ending work sat propped up at the well as she ran back into town and raved about Jesus, the man who knew how to meet her deepest need.

I wonder what Jesus would say to me if I had met him at that well. . . .

Would he have replaced the word "husband" with something else? Would he talk about my incessant desire to look impressive, that longing that leads to the kind of boasting that usually comes from the mouth of an insecure first grader and not from the lips of a middle-aged Christian man? Would he explore why I so often compare myself to others, desperately hoping to be more than mediocre, especially in the eyes of others?

Would he come to the same place with me as he did with that woman? "Mike, I am he. I'm the one you're looking for. I can fix that nagging feeling in your heart. I can quench the thirst in your soul. I can get you to GOD."

What would Jesus say to you?

Would he discuss your obsession with success, that moving target that never lets you sit down and enjoy a day off? Or would he bring up your love for money, which has doubled since you were sixteen but has not made you twice as happy? Would he ask you about your image, which costs you so much sweat and so many one-click clothing purchases but leaves you insecure whenever someone younger, skinnier, or prettier walks into the room?

I have a hunch he would encourage you to set down your jar, whatever shape it is, and worship the One who can finally, ultimately, and emphatically quench the thirst of your soul.

GOD is a spring of living water. His love is oceanic—immense and enough. And Jesus is the way that water gets into your soul.

Or, to use another biblical metaphor, Jesus is the only way to deal with the hunger in your heart.

$200 Sushi and Your Hunger for GOD

Back in 2015, my wife and I planned a vacation to Vancouver to experience a few days of "This!" with our northern neighbors. She, being the passionate planner of our travels, checked out a few tourist books on the city and made a list of must-dos for our trip.

That's when we heard about Tojo.

Hidekazu Tojo is one of the best sushi chefs on the planet. If you have ever eaten a California roll, you have tasted what is believed to be one of his original recipes. The *Wall Street Journal* once listed him in the top ten greatest preparers of raw fish on this earth.

Many of Kim's tour books gave the same advice: Save up your money and go to Tojo's. Order the omakase, where the chef chooses the meal for you, and prepare to enjoy the best meal of your entire life.

So, we did.

With a price tag of $200 per person, we originally felt we couldn't afford it,* but I offered Kim a compromise. I promised to stop going out to eat for months until we saved up enough to pay for the epic meal. She agreed, so I swapped my laptop screen saver from my smiling daughters to a headshot of Mr. Tojo.†

---

* Because my savings account went hevel when I had kids who, selfishly, didn't want to eat packaged ramen for every meal.

† Those who consider me a bad father for this move have never eaten at Tojo's.

Finally, the day came. We walked into Tojo's on our twelfth wedding anniversary and experienced, by far, the greatest meal of our lives. Tojo greeted us, his four-foot-and-a-few-inches frame making my short wife look like LeBron and me like Goliath, and then promised, "You are going to be happy."

We were.

Course after course demanded an obnoxious foodie photo to memorialize the master's creations. Plate after plate came out until our stomachs were begging for mercy, even as our taste buds begged for more. We toasted Mr. Tojo, snapped a picture with the legend, and prepared ourselves for the hefty bill.

But the host smiled and said, "Someone called last Friday and took care of it."

Huh?! "Who?" I asked, baffled.

"She said she didn't want you to know."[*]

Kim and I walked out the doors, laughing uncontrollably. The happiness over the experience, the food, the wine, and the surprise were more than our hearts could take in. "This!" "This!" "This!"

But less than an hour later, on the walk back to our hotel, some absurd words came out of my mouth. "Kim . . ."

"Yes, Michael?"

"I'm hungry."

Seriously. I said that. Double-digit minutes after eating the best meal of my entire life, I was hungry. My distance-runner metabolism processed Tojo's dishes and was ready for more. Apparently, the hunger of the human body is not easy to satisfy.

Nor is the hunger of your heart.

Both the stomach and the heart can enjoy incredible experiences yet still be hungry for more.

Just think of what we enjoy compared to the richest people of ancient times. Through work trips, vacations, or seventy-inch, super HD screens, we see the Pacific Ocean and the Grand Canyon

---

[*] "This!" This is a glimpse of the generous GOD who surprisingly pays the entire debt of our sin!

and Mexican beaches—stunning places that Jesus himself, in his earthly life, never once saw. Chicago, Minneapolis, and New York offer us cuisine from places King David never visited and people Solomon never knew existed. Free YouTube access at the public library offers every American the chance to see comedians, actors, and musicians better than those who filled the royal courts during the Ecclesiastes experiment.

We are spoiled, historically and globally.

So why is it so hard for us to stay happy? Why do we need another show, another trip, another night out, another pair of shoes, another phone, another screen, another car? Why do we go into debt to spoil our kids at Christmas and yet find them bored by New Year's Eve?

Just minutes after a feast, why do we say, "I'm hungry"?

Maybe because Someone put eternity in your heart. Maybe because GOD never wanted you to be completely content until you found the One you were created to crave.

Which is what Jesus told the crowd who came to his restaurant in Galilee.

In John 6, Jesus pulls off one of his most impressive miracles. He takes a little kid's lunch and feeds at least five thousand people. When the bill finally arrives, the crowd learns that Jesus has already picked up the tab. Understandably, the people like Jesus. They want more of his miracle bread. Free lunch has a way of making people happy.

But Jesus confronts their foolish thinking. He turns and teaches, "Do not work for food that spoils, but for food that endures to eternal life, which the Son of Man will give you" (v. 27).

What is the problem with food, even if Tojo or Chef Jesus prepares it? It doesn't last. GOD made your heart hungry for food that endures to eternity, so if temporary food is all you eat, you'll soon be growling for more.

Which is why Jesus suggested the Savior's Special. "Then Jesus declared, 'I am the bread of life. Whoever comes to me will never go hungry, and whoever believes in me will never be thirsty'" (v. 35).

Jesus knows his "never go hungry" and "never go thirsty" promises, unlike the temporary "food" of this life (purchases, compliments, dates, raises, etc.), stir up your heart like nothing else in this world can.

Why Celebrities Aren't Satisfied

But let's be honest for a second. Wouldn't you be happier if you had more of what this world has to offer? If you could afford a house on the water, an in-home chef, and a daily massage, wouldn't that be enough for a good life?

Not according to Mick Jagger. And Kendrick Lamar. And Woody Allen. And Alexander Hamilton. And U2. And Jim Carrey. And Trip Lee. And Tom Brady. And Bruno Mars. . . .

These people, despite their riches, fame, and success, have all admitted that the best this life has to offer is not enough to satisfy the soul.

Mick Jagger sang, "I can't get no satisfaction."[3]

Kendrick divulged he's "dying of thirst."[4]

In Woody Allen's *Midnight in Paris*, Gil admits, "Life's a little unsatisfying."[5]

Alexander Hamilton rapped,* "I've never been satisfied."[6]

U2 broke into the chorus, "But I still haven't found what I'm looking for."[7]

Madonna admitted, "Even though I've become Somebody, I still have to prove that *Somebody*. My struggle has never ended and it probably never will."[8]

Jim Carrey pulled back the curtain, saying, "I think everybody should get rich and famous and do everything they ever dreamed of so they can see that it's not the answer."[9]

Popular hip-hop artist Trip Lee shared about his experience with social media, "The main thing I want people to know is that no amount of likes really satisfies."[10]

---

*I'm not sure if the actual Alexander rapped these words, or if he rapped at all, but the Broadway version of him did.

Tom Brady confessed on *60 Minutes* after winning multiple Super Bowls, "It's got to be more than this. . . . This can't be what it's all cracked up to be."[11]

Bruno Mars sang of being sexually rejected, "You make me feel like, I've been locked out of heaven."[12]

The Roman poet Horace wondered, "How comes it to pass . . . that no one lives content with his condition?"[13]

His philosophical neighbor Cicero lamented that every person "sets out to be happy [but] the majority are thoroughly wretched."[14]

The Foo Fighters rocked, "Nothing satisfies, but I'm getting close."[15]

Markus Persson, the founder of Minecraft, tweeted his frustration after buying a $70 million mansion and living large as a thirtysomething. "Hanging out . . . with a bunch of friends and partying with famous people, able to do whatever I want, and I have never felt more isolated."[16]

And now you know why. While we might assume that ten thousand likes or coming home to Gisele* would be enough to satisfy, it turns out that GOD has set eternity in celebrity hearts too. Like Solomon's, their stories warn us that getting more money/attention/fame/power/whatever will not give us the happy life we imagined.

Either the blessing itself disappears or, despite its presence, it doesn't feel as good as it once did. In other words, the blessing always turns out to be less satisfying than GOD.

The prophet Isaiah once asked, "Why spend money on what is not bread, and your labor on what does not satisfy?" (Isaiah 55:2).

Why labor for more likes, more love, more fame, more fortune, or more of anything if, in the end, it cannot satisfy your soul?

Why work for "it" if "it" doesn't work?

Years ago, author C. S. Lewis chastised us all with his oft-quoted words, "We are half-hearted creatures, fooling about with drink and sex and ambition when infinite joy is offered us, like an ignorant

---

* The supermodel who married Tom Brady and gave birth to some of the planet's cutest kids.

child who wants to go on making mud pies in a slum because he cannot imagine what is meant by the offer of a [vacation] at the sea. We are far too easily pleased."[17]

The problem is not our desire for happiness or, as Lewis says, "infinite joy." Rather, our biggest problem is that we think too much of "This!" and too little of GOD.

Which leaves us singing, like the opera singer in *The Greatest Showman*, "Never enough for me."[18]

But how do you know when you have made the subtle shift from enjoying "This!" to needing it? What does a soon-to-be hungry, thirsty, unsatisfied soul look like?

To those questions we turn next.

STUDY QUESTIONS

1. Apart from GOD, whose presence has the most power to increase your happiness in life? How could that person help you seek GOD this month?

2. Read Ecclesiastes 1:1–11. Find three examples of the brevity of earthly blessings, then add three of your own from the past year of your life.

3. Reflect on this quote: "If we place our joy in something temporary, our joy will be temporary."

4. Read Psalm 63:1–8. Why does David claim that GOD's love is better than life?

5. Ask a teenager you know if they think celebrities are satisfied with their lives. Then ask them what they think is the secret to being satisfied. Share the concept of *hevel* with them as well as Solomon's experiment.

CHAPTER SIX

Sad Symptoms of Putting Your Hope in Hevel

If you have ever pulled a weed, you know the difference between tearing off the leaves and ripping out the roots. While the leaves might be the most visible part of the plant, the real problem is beneath the surface: the roots, which will produce another round of ugly leaves in no time.

In this chapter, I want to point out the "leaves" we might see in our lives that are all results of a deeper problem: putting our hope and happiness in temporary things.

1. Anxiety

Why do we get so anxious so often? Where does that nervous, uneasy feeling come from?

From forgetting that GOD is present even if "This!" isn't.

Let me explain this symptom with a few case studies.

DeAndre feels anxious about his new relationship. He really likes Kayla. But he has liked other girls in the past and those relationships didn't work out, so how can he be sure that this one will?

At times, he feels confident in their relationship, like when Kayla texts him in the middle of his workday with something funny. But when days go by and his phone never pings once, his heart rushes to worst-case scenarios about their future as a couple.

Why is DeAndre anxious? At first, we might say, "Because his relationship might not make it." But let's assume it doesn't work out for them. Isn't GOD still with him? If Kayla is what DeAndre *needs* to be happy, he's trying to fill the eternal part of his heart with a temporary girl. And, since even the best girls can't do that, anxiety is the most natural reaction.

Or take Stephanie. After putting in four years of dedicated work at an insurance company, she applies for a newly opened managerial role. Her boss and her boss's boss have always complimented her work, but there are some pretty talented (and younger) colleagues who also applied for the same position. For weeks, Stephanie anxiously checks her email, waiting for the word from her company.

Why is Stephanie anxious? We might say, "Because she really wants the promotion." But assuming she doesn't get it, isn't GOD still with her?

If GOD is a minimal source of happiness for Stephanie, she will need something else to fill that hole in her heart. And if that something else is as hevel as Solomon explained, then anxiety is to be expected.

Or think about Rebecca. She spends hours each day posing, filtering, posting, and connecting with her digital community. And she's good at it. She's a natural beauty with visible confidence and a keen sense of fashion, and people love Rebecca's pictures. Well, most people love most of her pictures. But she has learned that her family and friends are like a box of chocolates. She never knows what she's going to get. Sometimes only a few dozen people click their approval. On occasion, only a stray comment or two appears below her pictures. Rebecca knows the numbers, because she obsessively checks.

Why is Rebecca so anxious? At first we might say, "Because the encouragement of her friends and validation from her family means a lot to her." But we know that this kind of approval never lasts and the rejection will always haunt Rebecca. Doesn't GOD still treasure her, even if the entire internet ignores her?

If being liked by the GOD who created her seems small compared to the likes of her fellow creations, then Rebecca's joy depends on the click count, a number she can never count on. Which is the cue for anxiety to take center stage.

Anxiety is uncertainty. And everything is uncertain except for GOD.

In mathematical terms, the amount of your anxiety is directly proportionate to what you think of GOD. Think little of GOD, and your anxiety skyrockets and your soul chews its nails wondering if things will work out. Think much of GOD, and peace takes anxiety's place, since GOD is all you need.

So what makes you feel anxious? Where do your thoughts turn in the middle of class or during sleepless nights? Is it your financial future? Your dating prospects? Your ticking biological clock? How you compare to your older brother on the court or in the classroom? How you stack up to the last person who held your position in the company? How much of a difference you have actually made after five years at your job? Whether your cancer will come back? What will happen to our country? Whether your church is growing or your waistline is shrinking?

The good news is that GOD insists on being with you, even if you go bankrupt or get fired or need a tutor for your son. Even if you disappoint your boss or need another round of chemo, GOD will never leave you nor forsake you.

The bad news is that if you don't believe in a glorious and present GOD, his presence will not be powerful enough to give you peace. You will need something else, something that may or may not be there for you.

And anxiety will be your only logical conclusion.

A famous pastor once admitted that he used to puke before preaching. The thought of needing to impress his entire congregation Sunday after Sunday turned his stomach. He knew himself and his listeners well enough to know that some Sundays they nodded in appreciation while others they simply nodded off. So, week after week, his anxiety expressed itself in rather . . . well . . . visible ways.

The cure, he said, came when he read Colossians 3 and realized "Christ . . . is your life" (v. 4). Once his very life, his needed thing, was the certain Christ and not their uncertain applause, he could preach in peace.

Until his heart was satisfied in GOD, anxiety made him sick.

And until you remember "GOD is," anxiety will make you sick too.

2. OCD

In addition to your anxiety, thinking too little of GOD and too much of "This!" will lead to a dreadful spiritual condition that I call OCD—Obsessive Comparison Disorder.

If, instead of being satisfied that GOD is here, you constantly *need* that girl to pay attention to you, *need* your parents to applaud your achievements, *need* your boyfriend to approve of your beauty, *need* your classmates to be impressed by your humor, *need* your colleagues to praise your work ethic, or *need* any other type of affirmation, you will *need* to compare favorably to others. After all, no one notices the third-string quarterback or the run-of-the-mill employee. Only the best get the press.

Your happiness will hang on unending, obsessive comparisons: Did you sing better than the other students? Better than the other competitors? Did you play better than the other musicians? Better than the other performers at the local music festival? Did your video get more views? More than your last post? More than your peers'? Are you smarter than your older brother? Faster than your younger sister? Funnier than your best friend? Does your teacher or your boss notice that there's something special about you? Are you the best parent you can be?

On and on and on the comparisons go[*] for the sick soul searching for another hit of approval or praise, trying to replace that eternal hole with another square inch of "This!"

In contrast to the world, GOD is not looking for the best and the brightest. He is the GOD of the meek, the lowly, the poor, and the unlovely. "But God chose the foolish things of the world to shame the wise; God chose the weak things of the world to shame the strong. God chose the lowly things of this world and the despised things—and the things that are not—to nullify the things that are" (1 Corinthians 1:27–28).

The gospel is the only cure for our spiritual OCD. We don't have to compare ourselves to anyone when we remember that GOD's love comes with no strings attached and reaches down to the bottom to bless the ignored, the overlooked, and the unimpressive.

GOD is—even with those of us who don't get the world's praise. Forget that, and the obsessive comparisons will take your heart captive.

3. Exhaustion

A third sign that you've forgotten the power of GOD's presence is that you feel perpetually exhausted. You would love to sit down and rest, but you can't. You would take a day off and practice the Sabbath if you could, but it would cost you too much. So you choose life on a treadmill.

I once preached a sermon from a treadmill.

No joke. I grabbed an extension cord and powered up a treadmill in the center aisle of our church. I started off at a brisk walk during the introduction, accelerated into a decent jog at the halfway mark, and ended with a dead sprint for the climactic moment.[†]

---

[*] And on and on and on and on and on and on and on. . . . I know all too well, since I have a wicked case of OCD.

[†] You have never seen GOD's people so convinced they were about to witness a traumatic preaching injury.

As I spoke, I talked about how all too often we approach religion like it's an exhausting list of rules and rituals that we can never keep well enough, no matter how hard we try. If we're trying to sprint our way to salvation, we'll never get there. Many spend years on the religious treadmill until the day they burn out and quit.

Trying to satisfy the human heart apart from GOD is exhausting. And never ending. And dangerous.

If you try to satisfy that hunger in any way except through the belief that GOD is here, you will step onto a treadmill that will never let you rest. You will have to work to prove you are worth marrying (and then not divorcing), work to maintain your faithful friend status (even when your first kid arrives and you have zero time to give), work to get your colleagues' approval (a standard that only increases the more successful you are), work to get that college scholarship (and then the grades to keep it), work to stay strong and slim (even when your metabolism slows with age), work to be digitally successful (even though technology transforms the industry every few years), work to stay well-read (because thousands more books are published every year).

And then, after you are soaked with sweat from all that work, you will have to work some more. Because your girlfriend doesn't want a guy who *used to* plan romantic dates for her. Your friends don't want to remember the days you *used to* show up for drinks after the game. Your boss doesn't want to reminisce about the good old days when you *used to* make the company money. They all want you to do something now. So get back on the treadmill and get to work!

Have you ever felt that kind of exhaustion? You slave all day cooking meals, organizing schedules, making calls on your commute, returning emails promptly, taking the stairs, biting your tongue, offering helpful advice, working late, working out, picking up the kids, returning more emails while you cook more meals, praying, and reading, while trying not to fall asleep midsentence on GOD.

Without GOD's presence, a GOD big enough to quench your inner thirst and satisfy your heart's eternal hunger, you will end up a slave. Always running the race. Never reaching the finish line.

Always disappointing someone. Never enough for everyone. GOD is like a good shepherd who lets his flock lie down in peaceful pastures and nap beside quiet waters. But lose GOD and you lose the peace and the rest along with him.

I once heard a pastor say that your source of acceptance can't ever stop affirming you. Whoever you need to impress to feel like you matter will require you to work, but that work never ends. Or if it does, the affirmation does too.

Can I ask you a soul-searching question? Why do you do this to yourself? If you dig deep enough into your answers, I bet you don't think you could be happy if all you ended up with was GOD.

You need something more. And that need chains you to the treadmill life of trying to satisfy your own soul.

That is why I jumped off the treadmill. Midmessage, midsprint, I grabbed both handrails, and I jumped off the spinning track of death. Panting for breath, I flipped the power switch on the treadmill and told GOD's people about . . . GOD. The GOD who sent his Son to give us eternal life (John 3:16). The Son who ran the perfect race in our place (Hebrews 4:15). The Savior who cried, "It is finished" and then handed us the victory medal (John 19:30). The One who invited us to come to him and find rest (Matthew 11:28).

Exhaustion is a red light on the dashboard of your soul. And "GOD is" is the only way to fix it.

4. Disobedience

Jesus' simple invitation is "Follow me" (Matthew 4:19). He longs to take you by the hand and lead you into the very presence of GOD. But if GOD is not the place you truly want to go, Jesus isn't someone you're likely to trust.

Make no mistake, following Jesus will cost you a ton of "This!" If you think adulting* has its challenges, try obeying everything

---

* I think this is the trendy way to say going to work, paying bills, and not spending entire weekends on Mario Kart.

that Jesus commanded—and not just the convenient stuff you are already doing. Try letting him get the last word instead of your friends, family, or personal feelings. It will, no doubt, feel like you are carrying a cross. It will cost you the temporary highs that sin so often provides.

Like the acceptance of your roommates who feel judged now that you won't gossip with them like you used to. Or the temporary pleasures of looking at porn when she's not interested in sex. Or the short-term highs of buying more stuff when you prioritize GOD's goals in your budget.

Follow Jesus and your "This!" might be more temporary than ever.

Maybe this is why many people in our modern world say they love Jesus but are unwilling to sacrifice for him. We like what he is offering—life with GOD—but we don't like what he is taking—our here-and-now happiness. So, when he calls us to live counter-culturally, we rebelliously apologize, "I'm sorry, GOD, but I need 'This!' I can't be happy without it."

Think about your most common sins for a second. Even though I don't know what you do, I bet I know why you do it. You want more comfort, power, praise, acceptance, pleasure, attention, etc. And you realize that obeying Jesus' teaching will cost you some of that. So, you choose to sin.

But isn't GOD a greater source of comfort? Doesn't being part of his royal family give you a greater power? Isn't it enough that GOD himself pays attention to you every moment of every day?

See what I'm saying? Below the surface, sin is trying to replace GOD with something else out of a suicidal desire to be happy.

If I could turn this struggle into a math equation, it would be this: Your odds of following Jesus = What you think of GOD. Because if you think too little of GOD and too much of "This!", your odds of following Jesus are less than zero.

Only when GOD's presence becomes priceless to you will you give up any and every "This!" to get him (Matthew 13:44). Only when GOD becomes the only way to satisfy your soul will you give up money, fame, pleasure, approval, and anything else just to call on his name in faith (Acts 19:17–19).

And that is the very reason I became a pastor.

When I was in high school, I had every intention of pursuing a business degree from the University of Wisconsin–Madison. That's what my dad did. That's what my older brother did. That's what I was going to do.

Until I read Mark 8.

Jesus' life-and-death words grabbed my teenage heart and refused to let it go. "Then [Jesus] called the crowd to him along with his disciples and said: 'Whoever wants to be my disciple must deny themselves and take up their cross and follow me. For whoever wants to save their life will lose it, but whoever loses their life for me and for the gospel will save it. What good is it for someone to gain the whole world, yet forfeit their soul?'" (Mark 8:34–36).

I pondered how many people were living examples of the bad spiritual math that Jesus warned about in his message. Unwilling to lose "This!" in their lives, they were willing to lose Jesus. And they missed out on the life that Jesus was leading them to, an eternal life with GOD.

That day, I decided to become a pastor. Even if GOD used my life's work to change only one heart, to help one soul solve the math of eternity, I reasoned it would be worth it.

My passion for that passage has not changed.

Would you give up anything to be with GOD? If you had to lose eighty years of their approval and your comfort, would you do it? If following Jesus left you friendless apart from GOD's friendship, rejected apart from GOD's acceptance, and alone apart from GOD's presence, would you still follow him?

If not, you will eventually lose what your heart most desires. You will lose GOD.

But if you follow the Jesus who can get you to GOD, giving up everything is the most logical thing to do. After all, your loss is only temporary. Your gain is eternal.

Because you gain the eternal GOD.

5. Anger

The final sign that you think too little of GOD's presence is that you get angry at GOD when he takes away your "This!"

"GOD, how can you be loving if you let her die?" "How can you be real if you didn't answer my prayer?" "Why would I trust you if you couldn't even fix my marriage?" "Are you even out there?"

And it is so easy to get angry at GOD once "This!" is gone.

Which is why GOD put the book of Job in the Bible.

The Old Testament records the half-gripping, half-baffling story of a man named Job, a devout follower of GOD whose life was filled with "This!" GOD blessed Job with riches, a glimpse of the riches of heaven. And a wife, a glimpse of the affection between GOD and his people. And ten children, a glimpse of the fatherly love GOD has for his kids. And respect, a glimpse of the worth we will feel when GOD affirms our place in his kingdom. And health, a glimpse of the pain-free life that awaits us in the life to come.

And Job loved GOD. He praised his name. He worshiped him. He thought much of GOD.

But what would happen if GOD took away Job's "This!"? Would Job still love GOD? Or would he turn on him?

That was Satan's question for GOD. Job 1 records the devil's words: "'Does Job fear God for nothing?' Satan replied. 'Have you not put a hedge around him and his household and everything he has? You have blessed the work of his hands, so that his flocks and herds are spread throughout the land. But now stretch out your hand and strike everything he has, and he will surely curse you to your face'" (Job 1:9–11).

Satan claimed that Job never really loved GOD. Without a cushy and comfortable life, Job would spit in the face of GOD. Satan suggested Job, unlike David, who only wanted to seek GOD's face, only cared about the blessings that were in GOD's hands.

So, GOD mysteriously accepted Satan's challenge and put Job to the test. In a series of unspeakable tragedies, GOD allowed

Job's wealth and health and family to all turn to hevel. His flocks? Stolen. His employees? Lost. His children? Dead.

Job, understandably, was crushed. Yet what he said in the pit of his grief proved Satan wrong. "At this, Job got up and tore his robe and shaved his head. Then he fell to the ground in worship and said: 'Naked I came from my mother's womb, and naked I will depart. The LORD gave and the LORD has taken away; may the name of the Lord be praised'" (Job 1:20–21).

When Job lost his "This!", he continued to worship, declaring how much GOD was worth. He continued to praise the name of the Lord, saying good things about the GOD he believed in. Job didn't curse GOD to his face. Instead, GOD's face led Job to praise his name. Even in the grief. Even in the loss. Even in the grip of death.

I will let you read the rest of Job's fascinating story on your own, including his struggles to love GOD as his pain endured. If you make it through all forty-two chapters of Job, notice what got Job back on track—not a logical explanation of GOD's plan for his pain, but a personal encounter with the glorious Creator GOD.

But, for now, think of why GOD put that story in the Bible for us to read. I would suggest that Job's story is all of our stories. While you may not lose everything in one day, we all experience many moments when the Lord stops giving and starts taking away.

When that happens, do you think much of the GOD who allowed it? Do you run to GOD when there's nothing left, grateful that he is still present? Or does your reaction prove Satan's assumption about Job, that some people only love GOD because of what GOD gives?

This is what actually makes pain a gift. Without suffering, we would never know if we loved GOD for his presence or his presents. If GOD made your entire life easy, you would never have proof of whether your love for him was genuine. Maybe, like the kid whose grandma gives him serious cash each Christmas, you only stay in touch because you want some seasonal blessings.

So, what if GOD didn't give you any friends this year? What if no one who viewed your profile was romantically interested in you? What if no one was impressed with your work? What if you were overlooked or underappreciated despite your best efforts? What if chronic pain didn't leave you alone? What if GOD took away your health or your brother, your son or your daughter, your wife or your mother, your job or whatever? Would you still love and trust in him above all things?

When GOD stops giving and starts taking away, true faith is revealed. This is what Peter described in the opening of his letter, "These [trials] have come so that the proven genuineness of your faith—of greater worth than gold, which perishes even though refined by fire—may result in praise, glory and honor when Jesus Christ is revealed. Though you have not seen him, you love him; and even though you do not see him now, you believe in him and are filled with an inexpressible and glorious joy" (1 Peter 1:7–8).

This is the beauty of your pain. Every day that you suffer and yet talk to GOD and pray to GOD and cry to GOD and complain to GOD is a day that proves you believe in GOD! You love him even when his gifts are few. Even if the only gift left is himself.

But if ungrateful rage toward him replaces love for him, perhaps it's because there was no glorious GOD in our hearts to begin with.

Anxiety, comparison, exhaustion, disobedience, and anger. If you recognize one or more of these signs in your daily life, perhaps it is time to fix your eyes on the only thing that can give your heart lasting peace—the GOD who is still with you.

Christians Lie to Us

Unfortunately, when our friends and family see any of these signs in our lives, they rarely push us back to GOD's presence. Instead, even sincere Christians forget about GOD and overpromise a future with guaranteed "This!"

For example, your doctor suspects cancer and wants to run an MRI. When you anxiously share the news with the family, your brother says, "I'm sure it's nothing. God will take care of it." Others nod in agreement, hoping their positive outlook will ease your fears for the future.

But—can I be as honest as Solomon here?—it might not be nothing. It might be something. Something bad. Something deadly. Because your health is hevel too.

And, if it never gets better, will you still have hope? Will you die at peace in the presence of GOD?

Or your long-term boyfriend dumps you, leaving you angry at him and confused with GOD. Your best friend brings a bottle of wine to your apartment and listens compassionately as you cry. You're a mess, and she deeply wants to give you hope for the future. So she says, "I just know God has someone better in store for you. Give it a year and watch what God does."

But—will you hate me if I say this?—she can't guarantee that. GOD never promised significant others to all his sons and daughters. There might not be someone better. You might not find love again. You might die single, with a half-worn mattress and a collection of cats.*

Why do Christians do that so often? Why do we so optimistically make promises about other people's futures? How come Bible-believing people, who think Ecclesiastes is the trustworthy Word of GOD, don't trust the point of its passages that everything is hevel?

Perhaps because, deep down, it seems trite and shallow to say, "But even now, GOD is here!" We know it's what we are supposed to say, but it doesn't feel like enough to be helpful or hopeful. So, we grasp for something more. We try to help by pointing their hopes toward hevel.

But hevel can't offer hope at all.

---

* But don't be jealous. Cats can be glimpses of GOD too. And marriage is filled with more hevel than you think.

A Better Way to Live

These last few pages have been pretty depressing, huh?

For a book that is intended to increase your joy, I've slapped you around with a few truths that may have left you more discouraged than delighted.

I would say sorry about that, but I'm not that sorry.

Because I am in hot pursuit of your lasting happiness. I couldn't claim to care about you if I pushed you to place your hope in something temporary. So, before we could build your joy on a concrete foundation, we had to dig out the marshy soil in your soul. And like a construction project, it might have been messier and taken longer than you expected.

But now it's time to build something beautiful. Something strong enough to protect your peace when the storms blow through your life.

That something is a simple two-word phrase—GOD is!

GOD Is Not "This!"

Before I discovered the power of "GOD is," I was completely clueless about how often the Bible repeats the theme of GOD's presence. Although the wording varies from passage to passage, the big idea is the same—unlike all of the temporary things of life, GOD is always.

These days, nearly every devotional book and every worship song reminds me of one of GOD's greatest qualities: He always is!

I have already explained the beauty of remembering "GOD is like 'This!'" Now I want to explain the power of recalling, "But GOD is not like 'This!' 'This!' is temporary. GOD is eternal!"

Eight Biblical Ways to Say "GOD Is!"

Here are eight words that trigger my heart to remember that GOD is, right here, right now, and always:

1. Eternal—*Eternal* means "without end, lasting, permanent." It is the opposite of hevel, and it is the perfect word to describe GOD.

- "The eternal God is your refuge" (Deuteronomy 33:27).
- "Trust in the LORD forever, for the LORD, the LORD himself, is the Rock eternal" (Isaiah 26:4).
- "Now to the King eternal, immortal, invisible, the only God, be honor and glory for ever and ever. Amen" (1 Timothy 1:17).

Whenever I read the word *eternal* in the Bible, I remind my heart that GOD was, GOD is, and GOD will always be. He was here with me in my twenties, is now with me in my thirties, and will always be with me in the decades to come. He is the great I AM and never the retired I Was.

2. Everlasting—Just like the word *eternal, everlasting* distinguishes GOD from all the temporary blessings that don't last forever.

- "Stand up and praise the LORD your God, who is from everlasting to everlasting. Blessed be your glorious name, and may it be exalted above all blessing and praise" (Nehemiah 9:5).
- "But from everlasting to everlasting the LORD's love is with those who fear him" (Psalm 103:17).
- "And [Jesus] will be called Wonderful Counselor, Mighty God, Everlasting Father, Prince of Peace" (Isaiah 9:6).
- "The LORD is the everlasting God, the Creator of the ends of the earth. He will not grow tired or weary" (Isaiah 40:28).
- "The LORD appeared to us in the past, saying: 'I have loved you with an everlasting love'" (Jeremiah 31:3).

Like fresh donuts in the break room, nothing seems to last long in this world. Except GOD. GOD is always present with us. Because of Jesus, his love for us, acceptance of us, and affection for us is everlasting.

3. Unfailing—GOD doesn't give up, give out, or grow old. GOD is constant, steady, and reliable.

- "But I trust in your unfailing love; my heart rejoices in your salvation" (Psalm 13:5).
- "I have always been mindful of your unfailing love and have lived in reliance on your faithfulness" (Psalm 26:3).
- "How priceless is your unfailing love, O God! People take refuge in the shadow of your wings" (Psalm 36:7).
- "Within your temple, O God, we meditate on your unfailing love" (Psalm 48:9).

That last passage reminds me of the gorgeous auditorium at Fox Valley Lutheran High School in Appleton, Wisconsin. Towering high above the stage is an intricate piece of woodwork engraved with the words of Psalm 48:9, "Within your temple, O God, we meditate on your unfailing love." Whenever I sit down in that auditorium, I do just that.

My love often fails. My wife's love sometimes fails. Love from my family, friends, and kids is sporadic and uncertain. But GOD's love is as unfailing as his presence. It always is. And that is absurdly good news.

4. Enduring—To *endure* means "to stick around, to last, to be persistent and permanent." Like GOD.

- "Give thanks to the LORD, for he is good; his love endures forever" (1 Chronicles 16:34).
- "People, despite their wealth, do not endure; they are like the beasts that perish" (Psalm 49:12).

- "For the LORD is good and his love endures forever; his faithfulness continues through all generations" (Psalm 100:5).
- Read Psalm 136, which repeats the phrase "his love endures forever" twenty-six times!

Our family often says this prayer before dinner: "Come, Lord Jesus, be our guest, and let these gifts to us be blessed. Oh, give thanks unto the Lord, for he is good. His mercy endures forever."

I used to rattle off that prayer on autopilot, but now those words make me think so much about GOD. I consider "these gifts"—the food, the family, the time to actually eat a family dinner. I thank GOD for all of "This!", but I know that these gifts will not endure. The meal will end. We will soon go our separate ways. I will be hungry by 7:15 P.M.

But GOD is so good! Why? "His mercy endures forever." GOD's willingness to not treat me as my sins deserve will last long after the dishes are washed and dried. Pick a time, any time, and GOD's mercy will be there.

5. Always—*Always* means "without fail, consistently, 24/7/365."

- "Be my rock of refuge, to which I can always go; give the command to save me, for you are my rock and my fortress" (Psalm 71:3).
- "Yet I am always with you; you hold me by my right hand" (Psalm 73:23).
- "A loving doe, a graceful deer—may her breasts satisfy you always" (Proverbs 5:19).*
- "The LORD will guide you always; he will satisfy your needs in a sun-scorched land and will strengthen your frame" (Isaiah 58:11).

---

* Okay, I just wanted to see if you were still reading all these passages.

- "And surely I am with you always, to the very end of the age" (Matthew 28:20).

Bon Jovi once promised his lady he'd always be there with her.[1] With all due respect to the esteemed Mr. JBJ, I have a hunch that he didn't. I bet he sometimes left his girl alone when he went on tour. And I'd bet he was sometimes a total toolbox to her even when he was home, like every husband sometimes is to his bride. But GOD always loves, always guides, and always is here for us.

6. Never—*Never* means "not ever, at no time, not even once." GOD never fades or fails, even if everything else in life does.

- "Heaven and earth will pass away, but my words will never pass away" (Matthew 24:35).
- "Whoever drinks the water I give them will never thirst. Indeed, the water I give them will become in them a spring of water welling up to eternal life" (John 4:14).
- "Then Jesus declared, 'I am the bread of life. Whoever comes to me will never go hungry, and whoever believes in me will never be thirsty'" (John 6:35).
- "God has said, 'Never will I leave you; never will I forsake you'" (Hebrews 13:5).

When I prepare couples for marriage, I make them study the 10 Commandments of Communication, a list I created based on the biggest mistakes people make when talking with or listening to one another. The second commandment on that list is "Never say never," since this exaggeration is a conversational terrorist that blows up a healthy exchange of ideas ("You never listen to me!" "Never? Oh really? Then what was I doing for two hours last night?!").

But GOD is allowed to break my commandment. GOD's "nevers" are not exaggerations but expressions of his eternal character. GOD will never abandon you. GOD will never leave you. GOD's promises will never fail you.

Which means you will never live a minute without being loved.

7. Remain—To *remain* means "to stick around, to not leave, to last." Due to his eternal character, GOD remains with us.

- "They will perish, but you remain; they will all wear out like a garment" (Psalm 102:26).
- "But you remain the same, and your years will never end" (Psalm 102:27).
- "If we are faithless, he remains faithful, for he cannot disown himself" (2 Timothy 2:13).
- "He is the Maker of heaven and earth, the sea, and everything in them—he remains faithful forever" (Psalm 146:6).

There is a beautifully repetitive song that we sing at our church entitled "One Thing Remains." I am a tentative hand raiser in worship,* but these lyrics lift my hands up to GOD. "One thing remains . . . your love."[2]

Yes! The only thing that can satisfy my soul is the GOD who remains. GOD has set eternity in my heart, and I will never have enough until his eternal, lasting love fills me up.

8. Faithful—To be *faithful* means "to be dependable, trustworthy, or constant." Too often, people break their promises. But GOD is faithful.

- "I have always been mindful of your unfailing love and have lived in reliance on your faithfulness" (Psalm 26:3).
- "Your love, LORD, reaches to the heavens, your faithfulness to the skies" (Psalm 36:5).
- "But you, LORD, are a compassionate and gracious God, slow to anger, abounding in love and faithfulness" (Psalm 86:15).

---

* Lutherans actually have concrete in their hands, which makes them nearly impossible to raise in worship. Don't be mad at us, people. That's just how gravity works.

- "Not to us, LORD, not to us but to your name be the glory, because of your love and faithfulness" (Psalm 115:1).

As a father, I am so often unfaithful. I promise my kids we will play volleyball in the driveway, but then dinner takes too long, the sun sets, and I break my promise. I say I will give them my full attention, and then my device-addicted brain has me reaching for my phone.

But our Father is not like their father. What he says, he does. When he says he will always be with you and never take back his unfailing love for you, he means it. After all, his faithfulness tops the trees, soars past the birds, and reaches to the heavens.

Eternal. Everlasting. Unfailing. Enduring. Always. Never. Remain. Faithful. These eight words can trampoline your thoughts up to the greatest thought of all: GOD is. I encourage you to listen for them in Christian songs and watch for them on the pages of Scripture. The Holy Spirit salted the entire Bible with *is* so that you could taste and see that the Lord is good.

Once you savor and believe that, you are inching close to the abundant life that Jesus wanted you to have. Just ask King David, who described "GOD is" with a metaphor so powerful it deserves its own chapter.

STUDY QUESTIONS

1. Which of the five symptoms hit closest to home? Explain your answer.

2. Most social media posts are fueled by obsessive comparison disorder. How have you seen this in your life?

3. How might a more glorious view of GOD be the key to saying "no" to the opportunities that drive you to exhaustion?

4. Read Mark 8:34–38, the words that inspired me to become a pastor. Some have called this the most offensive thing in the Bible to twenty-first-century Americans. Why would that be? Why is a massive view of GOD necessary to follow Jesus?

5. Which of the eight ways to describe "GOD is" brought you the most comfort? Write your answer on a sticky note and put it in a prominent place in your room.

CHAPTER SEVEN

Life in the Refuge

King David knew where to find life that lasts. You might remember David, the warrior/king/shepherd/poet from the Old Testament who penned more than seventy psalms. But you might not be aware that David's works have a life-giving theme—"GOD is" our refuge.

Even though it was his son, Solomon, who later wrote Ecclesiastes, David too realized that life on earth, even for a child of GOD, was not always cupcakes and unicorns. That is why he publicly lamented his almost daily loss of "This!", detailing the injustice he suffered at the hands of power-hungry men. Refusing to paste on a spiritual grin, David cried and complained and called out to the name of his GOD. David didn't use Solomon's favorite word, but he was all too aware that everything in this life is hevel.

Except GOD.

David adored and worshiped and exalted and sought and saw GOD. His heart urged him to seek the face of GOD more than anything in life, and, as he did, he discovered a reason to rejoice always and a peace that goes beyond understanding. Because no matter how many good things his enemies snatched out of his hands, they could not touch David's best thing—GOD. GOD's presence became his refuge, his fortress, and his strength. David always came back to "GOD is" to find peace and restore his joy.

In order to appreciate David's poetry, picture this: You are a simple farmer in ancient Israel with a small plot of land and a family you adore. But, one day, you see a cloud of dust on the horizon, and soon the sun glints off of a thousand swords and shields.

The Philistine army.

Your family doesn't stand a chance with pitchforks and farming tools, so your only choices are to hide or die. So you scoop up your twin daughters, Hope and Life, in your arms. You demand your sons, Contentment and Joy, keep up with your stride. And you run.

The Philistine war cries grow louder, and your children start to cry in fear.

But then you hear a voice say, "Over here! Quickly!"

You turn to see a man desperately waving his arms, inviting you through a city gate. With no other option but death, you urge your children toward him. Contentment and Joy sprint on their little legs and enter first. You follow, carrying Hope and Life past the walls.

"Hide in there!" the man commands, pointing to an imposing tower built in the middle of the city. You obey, rushing the kids through the entrance and up the stairs.

The man immediately swings the thick door shut and bars it behind you.

Gasping and grateful, you look around with wide eyes. "What is this place?"

The man smiles. "This is our refuge."

In the ancient world, a refuge was the safest place to hide. Built in the centers of key cities, these towers had the thickest, strongest, most impenetrable walls. Sometimes called a fortress or a stronghold or a hiding place, it provided safety and peace. The enemies could destroy your home, maybe even break through the city walls, but they could not get into the refuge.

Imagine some frustrated Philistine standing outside the thick stone walls of the refuge with only a dinky spear in his hand. What is he going to do? Chip away at the rocks until he can poke his spear through? Take a running start and bust through the barricaded door?

Not a chance.

In a world without helicopters, drones, or grenades, there was nothing like a refuge to keep you safe and sound.

Run to the Refuge

Sometimes in my hospital visits or counseling sessions when people are facing cancer or a possible divorce, I draw a picture of a city with a refuge. In place of the four walls, I list the names of all the "This!" that may not be present in the days to come: their health, finances, marriage, and reputation.

I tell my dear brothers and sisters that I cannot guarantee those blessings will survive in the future. Cancer and infidelity are cruel enemies that ruthlessly murder so many of GOD's good gifts. If their reason for living is in those walls, they might not have a reason to live.

But then I draw the fortress. The refuge. The stronghold. An aggressively scribbled square in the middle of the city. A place big enough for peace, hope, and life to hide inside.

I open my Bible, read the comforting words about where their Savior is during this suffering, and promise them, "No matter what happens, GOD is here. And that means love is here. Acceptance is here. Wisdom is here. Comfort is here. A plan is here. A reason to wake up tomorrow morning is here. Purpose is here. Someone is here at your side."

David drew this same picture with his poetry. When everything went to hevel in his life—when friends betrayed and kings pursued and plans fell through—David ran to his refuge, the place where everything would be okay, where his peace and joy could live another day.

That refuge was GOD. The GOD who gave him joy. The GOD who filled him with hope. The GOD who was his life.

Here's a tiny percentage of David's passages to prove it:

- "LORD my God, I take refuge in you" (Psalm 7:1).
- "The LORD is a refuge for the oppressed, a stronghold in times of trouble" (Psalm 9:9).
- "Keep me safe, my God, for in you I take refuge" (Psalm 16:1).
- "The LORD is my rock, my fortress and my deliverer; my God is my rock, in whom I take refuge, my shield and the horn of my salvation, my stronghold" (Psalm 18:2).
- "But my eyes are fixed on you, Sovereign LORD; in you I take refuge" (Psalm 141:8).

David's theme is a reminder of Jesus, the Savior who invites you to take refuge when everything in life is falling apart. Your personal finances or reputation at school are as instantly destroyable as a simple hut in front of a bloodthirsty army. That is why Jesus beckons you to run and take shelter in the safest place in the world, the presence of GOD.

Today you can hide your heart in a place where you are loved by GOD, invited by GOD, accepted by GOD, befriended by GOD, known by GOD, chosen by GOD, and valued by GOD.

Since the walls of this refuge are rock solid, you never have to wonder or worry that your joy, contentment, hope, or life won't make it. As long as GOD remains GOD (and not some hopeless god) and as long as that glorious GOD is with you (which the eternal, everlasting, enduring GOD always will be), then you will be okay. Actually, you will be much more than okay.

In the refuge of GOD's presence, you can experience the best blessings on earth.

Remember my presentation and the WWE wrestling grade-school teacher who destroyed the stuffed representation of joy? I wasn't done with our volunteer just yet.

As the crowd laughed at his antics, I drew their attention to my "refuge." I had lugged my cubic-foot, fireproof safe to the presentation and placed it on stage. Now, no one has ever mistaken me for a body builder, but I can assure you this thing was a beast that nearly broke my back when I huffed it up our basement stairs and loaded it into my van for the upcoming presentation. My Town & Country was riding low with that safe sitting in the trunk.

I asked our volunteer to prepare himself for round two with the stuffed animal. But, before the bell rang, I opened the safe and placed Joy inside.* Closing the inch-thick steel door, I turned to our aspiring Monday Night Raw fighter and told him to have at it. Demolish Joy. Drop another elbow. Kick her into the crowd.

But he just stared at me. He knew he couldn't. Joy was in a safe place. Even though she was so vulnerable, the walls that surrounded her were not.

I love that picture of GOD. That is the result of his glorious presence in your life.

You and I are so breakable. There are a thousand enemies in life that can steal our joy and murder our hope. But none of them is as strong as GOD. GOD has no crumbling towers, decaying gates, or aging bricks.

And because GOD is gracious and kind, he has a place in that refuge for you. He is inviting you today to hide your hopes, your happiness, your peace, your entire life in the safest place on earth.

---

* Which technically would have suffocated her to death, I know, but every analogy is flawed, so roll with me.

The walls of good mental health, satisfying work, and amazing friendships are not nearly as strong as any of us would like. The battering rams of this broken world break them down and kidnap the hopes and joys that are trembling inside.

Unless there is another place to hide. Unless we have a refuge to run to.

Eight Results of Life in the Refuge

What happens when we place all of our life in the refuge of GOD's presence? Just like there are signs in our lives that show when we have placed our hope in something temporary, our lives show the signs of a hope placed in our eternal GOD. Here are eight glorious results of believing that GOD is with us today.

1. Joy

Joy is the happiness of having GOD.

It's the relief you feel when you are sitting in the refuge, knowing that nothing can separate you from the GOD who loves you (Romans 8:38–39). It's the smile that spreads across your soul even during times of loss, because you know you cannot lose what matters most—GOD.

This is the middle ground that many Christians miss when it comes to biblical joy. Some equate it with worldly happiness that is dependent on an easy, pain-free life. Others neuter it of any happiness and make joy stoic and unemotional. But the Scriptures offer a nuanced definition of joy, one that is extremely emotional yet only dependent on the reliable presence of GOD.

Look at the joy David felt as he took refuge in GOD:

- "But let all who take refuge in you be glad; let them ever sing for joy. Spread your protection over them, that those who love your name may rejoice in you" (Psalm 5:11).

- "Taste and see that the LORD is good; blessed is the one who takes refuge in him" (Psalm 34:8).

- "But I will sing of your strength, in the morning I will sing of your love; for you are my fortress, my refuge in times of trouble" (Psalm 59:16).

- "The righteous will rejoice in the LORD and take refuge in him; all the upright in heart will glory in him!" (Psalm 64:10).

David is singing, rejoicing, trusting, loving, and breathing a sigh of relief. Why? Because his joy is hiding behind the impenetrable walls of GOD. He knows he is going to be okay. And you are too.

That's what I once told Katie, my dolphin-loving friend, when cancer T-boned her twentysomething life. Stage IV non-Hodgkin's lymphoma. The woman who cut my hair was about to lose all of hers. And it was very possible that she would lose so much more.

I remember visiting Katie in the hospital and walking with her family around the hospital halls. We found a private area near some sunny windows where we sat down on the floor to talk and pray. There, on the tile floor, I traced a big rectangle and told my friend about the refuge, the place where even cancer couldn't get in.

I knew Katie's hair and health and life were outside the walls. They were uncertainties in a world gone to hevel. So, I encouraged her to put her hope in the refuge, to remember the GOD who would always be there even if everything else was gone. No matter what the PET scan said or how successful the surgery was, GOD would be faithful to his "never leave you" promise.

Even more, I reminded her that our GOD is . . . GOD. He is glorious and satisfying and wonderful and worthy of praise. He is infinitely better than perfect health or a budget that isn't drained by months of medical bills. Whatever she lost was nothing compared to the GOD she could not lose.

If GOD was her source of joy, then she would always have a reason to rejoice.

You might not be battling cancer today, but the same message is true for you. Your joy can cling to the stubborn promise that every spiritual blessing is yours within the refuge. Jesus has opened the door so that the cravings of your heart can always be satisfied with the promises of GOD.

When your father's affection isn't, GOD is.

When your mother's attention isn't, GOD is.

When your brother's character isn't, GOD is.

When your teacher's fairness isn't, GOD is.

When your school's protection isn't, GOD is.

When your friend's trustworthiness isn't, GOD is.

When your boyfriend's faithfulness isn't, GOD is.

When your body's strength isn't, GOD is.

When your financial stability isn't, GOD is.

When your spouse's love isn't, GOD is.

When your son's appreciation isn't, GOD is.

When your life's ease isn't, GOD is.

When your walls come crumbling down, when your "This!" is disappearing like vapor in the wind, whenever life is drop-kicking your joy, whenever something good isn't, GOD is.

And he is GOD! The most thrilling, satisfying, peace-giving, joy-increasing, heart-pumping person imaginable is with you. And he always will be.

2. Hope

The second result of making GOD your refuge is hope.

We all know the power of hope. Hope gave Holocaust captives a reason to stay alive. Hope keeps spouses from punching out and giving up on their marriage. You can go through almost anything as long as you have hope.

But, sadly, we often misuse that beautiful word. Think of the common ways we use *hope* in our conversations—"I hope the

Packers make the playoffs this season." "I hope to have grandkids soon." "I hope Justin Timberlake delivers some sausage sandwiches for breakfast."*

What does hope mean in each of those sentences above? Nothing more than "I want" or "I'd prefer" or "I'd like." But, by this point, you know all too well that wishes and wants are all hevel, temporary and uncertain. Which means that this type of hope isn't very hopeful.

Thankfully, there is a better kind of hope. The biblical kind. I define hope as "a for-sure future." Something that might not be here just yet, but is absolutely guaranteed to be there in the future. Something you don't have to pace or fret or worry about, like the weather forecast or the Packers' divisional record. In other words, biblical hope is the guarantee that GOD will be there for you tomorrow. If GOD is everlasting, eternal, faithful, and trustworthy, then he will be with you in the days to come. It's your for-sure future!

David expresses his hope like this: "God is our refuge and strength, an ever-present help in trouble" (Psalm 46:1).

As far as hyphenated phrases go, that is one of my favorites. GOD is not a maybe-present help or a possibly present help. He is an ever-present help.

That's hope.

Which is why you can talk trash to the devil.

The devil can tempt you, lie to you, slander GOD, throw a fit, and try to scare you at night. But he can't touch your hope. He can't change the fact that "GOD is" with you, here and now. And GOD will surely be with you tomorrow when your boss "wants to talk" and next Tuesday when you have your annual checkup and in six weeks when you have to show up for court and on the next national election night and . . . well, all the days and hours and minutes and seconds that are packed into your future.

In other words, your worst-case scenario is that you end up with just GOD.

* What? A guy can hope, right?

The devil hates it when you hold on to hope like that. When your heart takes a nap inside the refuge because you know nothing can threaten GOD's presence in your life. When your hope is happily whistling behind those unbreakable walls.

Oh, the enemy howls like a hurricane wind. He can lie all day, but he can't pick the lock. Your soul is safe when GOD is with you.

Listen to how the apostle Peter put it: "Praise be to the God and Father of our Lord Jesus Christ! In his great mercy he has given us new birth into *a living hope* through the resurrection of Jesus Christ from the dead, and into an inheritance that can never perish, spoil or fade. This inheritance is kept in heaven for you, who through faith are shielded by God's power until the coming of the salvation that is ready to be revealed in the last time. In all this you greatly rejoice" (1 Peter 1:3–6, emphasis added).

Why can you "greatly rejoice," even if you are suffering in this life? Why should you praise GOD today, even if your body hasn't been operating at full strength in years? Because you have a living hope. You have a for-sure future in Jesus Christ. You have an inheritance that can never be taken away (sounds like a refuge, right?). You have something stored in heaven for you that the devil himself cannot heist.

That something is seeing the face of GOD. His glorious face is the Christian's for-sure future.

That kind of hope is what I use to raise the spirits of my co-workers at Time of Grace, the media ministry I am a part of. At times, we have to wrestle with tough decisions about how to use our limited time and resources. Should we try this or that? Should we spend our time focusing on this initiative or that one? Will people be excited to support this, or will we end up short?

Sometimes our meetings get pretty serious as we consider everything that is at stake. Which is when I smile and express my unshakable hope, saying something like, "Well, if this goes south, we might fall behind on our budget. And if we fall behind on our budget, we might have to downsize our team. And if we downsize our team, some of us might lose our source of income and our insurance. And if we lose our incomes, we might be left with just GOD."

That is a pretty sweet worst-case scenario!

This may sound flippant, maybe even casual, but it's the truth, and we know now that believing anything else is a lie that will only lead to disappointment and pain. Of course we work hard, we do all we can to steward the opportunities and responsibilities GOD has given, but in the end, GOD is our hope.

I "hope" it inspires you too.

"We have this hope as an anchor for the soul, firm and secure. It enters the inner sanctuary behind the curtain, where our forerunner, Jesus, has entered on our behalf" (Hebrews 6:19–20).

Our souls are anchored, firm and secure, in the presence of GOD, which Jesus opened through his death and resurrection. So, take hope, brothers and sisters; your soul is safe with GOD.

3. Peace

The Hebrew word for *peace* means "to be whole." When you have everything you need to rejoice right now, you have arrived at *shalom*, a deep sense of spiritual peace. We can only have the hope of wholeness when our hope is in the Holy One.

When I was thirty, I stood atop one of the most impressive fortresses on earth—Masada. If you have never heard of it, Google it now and gasp as you see one of Israel's most popular tourist attractions. Perched atop a rocky plateau, Masada was built by Herod the Great in the 30s BC to keep him safe in times of war and trouble.

From inside the fortress, you feel invincible. What foe could possibly climb hundreds of feet up the rocky cliffs while rocks and spears rained down from above? No wonder the Jewish rebels ran to Masada in AD 70 to take their last stand against the Romans.

Even Masada Was Hevel

But guess what? Masada wasn't a reliable refuge.

The Romans stacked a massive pile of rocks along one of the cliffs of Masada, turning the impossible climb into a fairly steep but still climbable hill. Pushing their towers and weapons of war up the incline, the Romans busted through the walls and destroyed the refuge.*

On a windy afternoon, I spoke to a small crowd gathered on Masada's plateau. I retold the story of the rebels' last stand and the Romans' patient plan to breach the walls, a reminder that everything in this life can fail, even the "walls" we imagined would stand forever.

And then I read the words of Psalm 46. "[GOD] says, 'Be still, and know that I am God; I will be exalted among the nations, I will be exalted in the earth.' The LORD Almighty is with us; the God of Jacob is our fortress" (Psalm 46:10–11).

---

*The heartbreaking ending of the story is that the defeated Jews committed mass suicide before the Romans got through the walls.

131

The key to sitting still, to having peace, is to know that the Lord is GOD. Exalted, meaning GOD, not God or god. With us, meaning GOD is here, not that he was or will be. That is our fortress, the place our hearts run to and hide in. The place no Roman army or modern enemy can destroy.

Are you sick of running around, trying to find the peace that will make your heart whole? Trying to find the one person or purchase or cause or look that will give you a lasting sense of being complete? There's only one place to find peace like that: GOD's presence. Remember that GOD is with you. What your heart needs to be complete—love, forgiveness, friendship, approval, worth, purpose—it has, right now, because of GOD's willingness to be by your side. Inside the walls, GOD gives you every spiritual blessing your soul needs to be whole and at peace.

This is the peace that David found in Psalm 23, which is probably the most famous song in human history. It is a touching source of hope for the dying, and at nearly every funeral I have ever attended, the words of Psalm 23 have been spoken, sung, or sermonized.

But David wrote Psalm 23 for the living too.

Think about his lyrics in light of what we have learned about pain, uncertainty, and the unfailing promises of GOD's presence:

> The Lord is my shepherd, I lack nothing. He makes me lie down in green pastures, he leads me beside quiet waters, he refreshes my soul. . . . Even though I walk through the darkest valley, I will fear no evil, for you are with me. . . . You prepare a table before me in the presence of my enemies. . . . My cup overflows. Surely your goodness and love will follow me all the days of my life, and I will dwell in the house of the Lord forever.
>
> Psalm 23

David didn't have a pain-free life. He mentions "the darkest valley" and "the presence of my enemies." And yet David felt a sense of peace, "I will fear no evil," and shocking contentment, "I lack nothing."

And why? Not just because he would one day, far in the future, dwell in GOD's house forever. But also because, as David sang, "You are with me." Not "was" or "might be," but "are." Present tense. GOD is here.

With Jesus as your good shepherd, guiding and leading, you do not have to be afraid. You are always and eternally loved and accompanied and invited to the table. The cup of your contentment and happiness can overflow because a good and loving GOD is following you through every stage of life.

So, in the midst of all the uncertainties of this day, sing David's song. Remember "GOD, you are with me." And you will lack nothing. You will have peace.

4. Fearlessness

Fear is the unpleasant suspicion that something bad might occur. It's the angst that if _____ happens, then you will lose _____.

But if GOD's constant presence in our lives means that we will never lose him, we do not have to fear whatever fills that first blank.

If GOD is your refuge and strength, an untouchable and ever-present help in trouble, what might you be afraid of? Who or what could take away the soul-satisfying GOD who is all you need to have joy, hope, and peace? Answer: No one and nothing.

In my office is a picture of Jesus, painted by the friend of a friend. Displayed next to Jesus is a piece of Father's Day art that my girls created when they were barely potty-trained. It's a finger-painted masterpiece with a passage from Psalm 27:1, "The LORD is the stronghold of my life—of whom shall I be afraid?"

Since I'm an aspiring minimalist, I have tossed most of the crafty Father's Day gifts from over the years,* but this one I have kept, because one glance reminds me why I never need to be afraid of

---

*Does that make me a terrible father? Because, seriously, I can only handle so much Popsicle-stick art. . . .

anything. No unexpected email or work drama or family struggle can bust through the walls of GOD and take away his eternal love for me.

You don't need to steal my painting to find the same fearless life. Confront your fears with the same promise and preach to your own heart, "But GOD will be with me." Tell your anxious mind that no matter what, GOD is here. Attempt to fill in the blanks. Even if the worst thing happens, the actual worst thing—losing GOD—cannot happen.

When you fear a worst-case scenario with your health or the upcoming job cuts or the consequences of a poor choice you made and cannot change, ask a simple question, "Can this take away my GOD?"

I don't know your fears, but I know the answer to that question: Not a chance!

This is the fearless factor of the Christian faith. The more you fear GOD, the less you fear everything else. For you math lovers, I would say it like this: There is an inverse relationship between

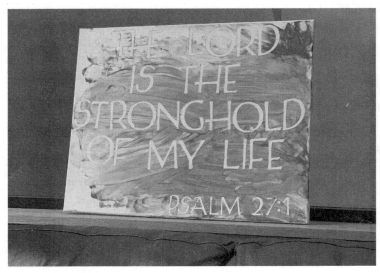

The Secret to Satisfaction

the fear of GOD and the fear of life. When the former goes up, the latter goes down.

When I stop believing in a small god, I start seeing a glorious GOD. And once I understand how GOD is more than enough to satisfy my heart, my only true fear would be to lose GOD. And since that ain't happening, why would I be afraid?

Outside the walls, your dreams and wants and preferences might die, but inside the walls your hope is alive and well. Because GOD still is.

Eventually, like David, you can boast in your refuge, "The LORD is the stronghold of my life—of whom shall I be afraid?" (Psalm 27:1).

5. Gratitude

Once you come to accept that everything except GOD is temporary, hevel, you can marvel at the fact that so many temporary things are here. Although they might be gone tomorrow, our generous GOD gave them to you today.

As wiser folks have said, count your blessings. Your soul didn't need them, yet GOD still chose to give them.

So many parts of your body could have broken down and left you crippled on the couch, but today you feel good enough to go to school or head off to work or play in the backyard with your kids. So many people in your life could have complained about your work this week, but it's Thursday and your inbox is empty of angry emails. Your daughter could have been friendless, but she spent both recesses laughing with a classmate. Your father, like so many others, could have abandoned you, but instead he was there at Thanksgiving dinner (even if his political opinions were a bit much . . .). Your basement could have flooded during the storm, but GOD kept it dry. You could have been scarred by your church experience, but you grew up with hundreds of Jesus-centered Sundays. You could have ended up broke, but here you are buying a four-dollar pumpkin spice latte. You could have been homeless or jobless or penniless, but you have a roof and a boss and a bank account.

Knowing "This!" is so temporary makes the Giver of every "This!" even more glorious.

So when the walls of good health, good friends, and good days are standing, thank GOD that he gave you even more than the refuge you need to rejoice.

The other night, I came home late from my indoor soccer games to find my two daughters fast asleep. Turning on the hallway light, I crept into my youngest's room and saw her half-buried in a pile of sloth-related paraphernalia. Wearing homemade sloth pajamas. Head buried into her sloth-themed pillowcase. Surrounded by all five of her sloth stuffed animals.*

There she lay with one bare foot sticking out from the covers. I grinned like only a dad can and thought, *"This!"* If this sight makes me so happy, what will I feel when I see the One who created those pigtails and that little foot?

So, I decided to sit down on the carpet next to her bed. Silently, I stared at those not-so-little-anymore toes hanging off the edge of her mattress, and I felt so grateful.

"GOD," I prayed, "she's still here. You never promised she would live this long, but she's still here. You gave me another night with this incredible kid. Thank you."

Perhaps, instead of being angrily surprised when something temporary turns out to be temporary, we could be surprised at all the temporary blessings that GOD extended into another day.

6. Selflessness

The sixth result of life in the refuge is the ability to live a selfless life.

Here's the logic: If being with GOD is all that I need to make me whole, I don't need to selfishly use you to satisfy my heart. In-

---

* She's currently in a 12-step program for sloth addiction. Thank you for your prayers.

stead, I am free to use my gifts to serve you, to give you a glimpse of the GOD who is always with me.

Raising kids or teaching preschool or working second shift as a nurse doesn't mean you are selfless. You might be using your position to fill that void in your heart—you need to be needed so your peers validate your importance; you need to impress your students (and their parents and your principal and your colleagues) so that you are praised as somebody special; you need frequent appreciation from your kids or you'll consider your work worthless.

In other words, you might be in the "service industry," but that doesn't make you a servant.

This is a massive struggle for me, even as a man in ministry. According to the StrengthsFinder personality test, two of my top five strengths are Significance and Competition. This means that I deeply long to do something that matters in this life and that I instinctively compare myself to others.* The GOD-given gift of these strengths is that I long to do something that matters in the eyes of GOD, like see lives changed by the love of Jesus, and that turning anything into a competition is an instant source of motivation.† The very, very dangerous weakness is that when I don't compare favorably, I can lose my joy instantaneously.

Most of the time, this temptation kills me. When I foolishly compare this Sunday's church attendance to last week's or the number of people baptized this year to last year's number, when fewer people read this blog post than the last one or came to this Bible class as compared to last semester. . . . Honestly, it's ugly. And I hate it. I battle deep thoughts of failure and inadequacy after I preach average messages, sometimes thinking I should quit midsermon because I am so terrible at what I do. My struggle is so

---

* If that sounds treacherous, it is. Please pray for my wife. And our church. And my soul.

† My bride has figured this out to her advantage. "Mike, I bet you can't fold the laundry in three minutes." "Oh yeah? I bet I can!" She's one smart cookie. . . .

bad that my friends pray for me before, during, and after church. Because I need it.

What is much worse than my lack of joy, however, is what that lack of joy implies. That GOD is not enough for me. That faithfully sharing Jesus with the few who showed up was not enough for me. That all of this gospel work is not really about GOD or others. It's about me.

That sucks to say.* But it's true.

But I remember one day that was gloriously different. That day with the WWE teacher and the stuffed animal in the safe. There I was speaking to one thousand of my colleagues at a conference on what later became the premise of this book. Normally, that kind of event would have murdered my joy and made me desperately anxious for their approval.

But, by the grace of GOD, something was different. As I waited to be introduced, I thought about GOD. I thought about his glory and his presence in the room. I tried to picture him, bursting with light and infinitely pleased with me, because I was his child through faith in Jesus.

I can still picture where I was standing in that auditorium when I said to myself, "I am good. I don't need anything. No matter what happens today, GOD will be here on the drive home."

That was one of the most joyful moments of my ministry. GOD freed me from needing people's approval, allowing every word I spoke to be about giving and not getting. My longing was to bless those in attendance, no matter how much positive feedback I got afterward.

It was a rare experience for me, but it was beautiful. I want more moments like that. I'd bet you do too.

Whether you are giving a presentation to the leadership team at work or getting ready for your solo at the choir concert, few things are as freeing as the glorious presence of GOD.

---

* If "sucks" feels like an inappropriate word, I am only using it to explain how inappropriate my heart can be.

So, before you stand up, before you serve, before you give, seek GOD. Remember that your heart is hidden in the refuge of GOD's presence. Put your hope and your postperformance, postpresentation future in GOD, the faithful Savior who will always accept you and never forsake you. Try to picture his expression, the face of a Father who is pleased with you, and preach to your heart the truth that his expression will not change. Because his love isn't earned. It's given freely.

Fill up your heart with GOD. Then you will be set free to serve.

Maybe we could pray for each other—author and reader—that we would both think so much of GOD that we would finally pour out our lives into selflessly serving others.

7. Boldness

The seventh result of life in the refuge is a boldness in sharing your faith with others. This is true in two ways:

First, we tend to talk about amazing things that make us happy. As Jesus said, "For from the overflow of the heart the mouth speaks" (Matthew 12:34 TLV). You don't have to guilt a young woman into talking about the new boyfriend who surprised her with flowers and a romantic date. And you don't have to twist a kid's arm to get him to bring up the pile of presents he opened on Christmas. Good news has a way of going public. Happy hearts won't be put on mute.

So, maybe one of the keys to evangelism is the *evangel*. That word, in Greek, literally means "good news." If Jesus has given us the priceless gift of being with GOD, and if that GOD makes us happier than any relationship or Christmas present, then maybe our happy hearts would overflow into words about GOD.

If we believe in some lame god or some stiff God, no wonder weeks go by without us speaking a word of his glory.

But if our habit of "This!" has allowed us to see GOD, then our peace will start to preach and our joy won't be contained to Sunday morning.

But there is a flaw with my comparisons, isn't there? Because few, if any, of the young woman's friends are going to feel awkward when she brings up the boyfriend. There is no cultural rule that says, "You shouldn't talk about politics or boyfriends in mixed company." And no one is offended by the annual recap of Christmas morning.

But people sometimes feel awkward when you bring GOD into the conversation. Your friends might reject the topic or change the subject or avoid you altogether. We would talk about Jesus more often, but his name might cost us their approval or their acceptance or their desire to hang out with us.

But GOD's presence is the key to fixing that too.

The second way in which the refuge can help you reach out is that you are freed from the fear of a negative reaction. No matter how people react to your love of Jesus, you will still have everything you need to rejoice and have peace. They might reject you, but GOD is here to accept you. They might avoid you, but GOD is here beside you. They might attack you, but GOD is here to defend you. They might think less of you, but GOD is here to delight in you.

So, whether their love for you grows or disappears like the mist, you won't end up with an empty heart. You will still have GOD.

And maybe, as the Holy Spirit works, they will want to join you in the refuge of GOD's glorious presence too!

8. Obedience

According to Jesus, loving GOD is the most important thing for GOD's people to do. And what does love look like? "Love the LORD your God and keep his requirements, his decrees, his laws and his commands always" (Deuteronomy 11:1). For Christ, love is not a warm fuzzy feeling. It's an emotion that expresses itself in obedience. But how do you end up with a love so strong that you are willing to say, "Your will be done"?

I suggest that seeing GOD is essential to obeying him.

If GOD commanded us to love him but was not himself inherently lovable, the commandment would be equally impossible and insulting. But if GOD opens our eyes to see him as he actually is, giving us minute-by-minute glimpses of his glory, then love, and obedience, would be the most obvious response.

This is the intersection of delight and discipleship. When you follow GOD and find everything your heart craves, you are finally ready to live for his name, his will, and his glory. So, before you seek the willpower to keep GOD's commandments, seek to see GOD and take refuge in him.

Pastor Bryan Chapell tells the story of the beautiful girl he fell for, Kathy, who would eventually become his wife. It was his first visit with her and her parents, and they enjoyed a picnic togegher on a beautiful autumn afternoon.

Then, as Bryan describes it, Kathy's "blond hair shone and her green eyes sparkled with the radiance of the day," and she asked him a simple question, Would he like to walk with her?

It was an easy question to answer.

As Dr. Chapell explained, this is how obedience works in Christianity. GOD asks us to walk with him, to obey him, but first he reveals his beauty and his glory. He opens our eyes to see his love and mercy.[1]

John famously put it this way, "We love because he first loved us" (1 John 4:19). Why do we love GOD enough to obey him? Because we have first seen his beautiful love for us at the cross of Jesus.

So, when GOD asks, "Want to obey me?" we don't have to think twice.

Yes, obedience to GOD will cost us earthly comfort, human approval, and a huge chunk of our time and money. But that is not where our deepest happiness is found. Once our eyes see GOD, our hands open to serve him. Because even if we had to give up everything else to obey him, we would still have him.

And he is all we need.

As the guy who saw Jesus face-to-face once put it, "This is love for God: to keep his commands. And his commands are not burdensome" (1 John 5:3).

Two Words Down, One to Go

Before we wrap up this chapter, let's think of the two life-changing words we have studied so far:

GOD—Thinking more of GOD is the key to truly living. That is why we leverage every "This!" (good moment) and every "That" (bad moment) to adore, exalt, glorify, magnify, lift up, love, fear, and worship the name of GOD. Or, as Jesus taught us to pray, "Hallowed be your name!" Nothing matters more than what we think when we think of GOD.

Is—We were created to hunger and thirst for something that always "is," for things that last. This is why, as so many celebrities have admitted, money, attention, and fame are too small and short-term to satisfy the human soul. Only GOD can fill that eternal hole in our hearts, because only GOD always "is." He is everlasting, enduring, unfailing, always abiding, never forsaking. That means his presence is our stronghold, the place where we can become the most joyful, hopeful, peaceful, fearless, grateful, selfless, bold, and obedient Christians on earth.

In a moment we will talk about the last life-changing word. But first, I would like to pause and pray.

A Prayer for GOD's Presence

There is a passage I pray almost every morning. I say "almost" because I am not a morning person. Some mornings I wake up in a groggy fit of snooze button–slamming anger at the GOD who is so frustratingly consistent with rotating the earth.

But eventually I compose myself and pray this powerful prayer. I can call it powerful without bragging, because I didn't come up with the prayer. Moses did. And Moses was a smart guy. He prayed, **"Satisfy us in the morning with your unfailing love, that we may sing for joy and be glad all our days"** (Psalm 90:14).

Those words are like Cinnamon Toast Crunch for my soul.* I can't get enough of the delicious connections between that prayer and what we have learned together.

Satisfy—GOD, I don't want to chase the wind and spend my life needing more money, more attention, more stuff, more likes, or more of anything. I want you to satisfy my heart.

In the morning—GOD, I don't want to wait for evening to be satisfied. I want to be content right now, at 10:17 A.M., after lunch, on the drive home, and throughout the day.

Sing for joy—GOD, make me so happy that I can't help but sing, like when a Metallica song comes on the radio and I crank it up so loud my daughters scream for mercy in the back of my car. I'm praying for an absurd amount of joy today, enough to make me sing.

Be glad—I don't want to mope around and wait to die to be happy. I want to be glad today, even if this day is difficult.

All our days—GOD, I don't want my gladness to end after today. And I don't want it all for myself. I am thinking of "our" days. My wife's day. My kids' days. My friends' days. My church's day. Bless us all, Father.

What an amazing prayer Moses wrote! But did you notice the part I skipped? It's what makes GOD our refuge and strength, an ever-present help in trouble. Moses prayed . . .

With your unfailing love—The only thing that can satisfy me right now and throughout the day, the only guaranteed source of joy and gladness for this day, the only non-hevel part of today is GOD's unfailing love.

Start every day in the refuge, and no matter where your waking hours take you, never step outside of it. And there, in the presence of GOD, find all the hope your heart needs in those two stunning words—GOD is!

---

* Which is one of the best "This!" moments I have experienced all week.

STUDY QUESTIONS

1. Draw your own copy of my map of ancient city walls with a stronghold inside at its center. Why is this concept so vital to your joy today?

2. Which "walls" have you seen fall down in your life? At the time, did you run to GOD as your refuge? Why or why not?

3. Read Psalm 46. What blessings are offered to those who make GOD their refuge?

4. Which of the eight results of life in the refuge do you long for the most? Spend some time in prayer asking GOD to give you this blessing as you seek his face today.

5. Memorize the words of Psalm 90:14 so that GOD's satisfying love is stored deep in your heart.

PART 3

GOD Is Here.

CHAPTER EIGHT

The Best "Here" We Ever Had

My favorite piece of my bookmark collection* is from Koh Samui, one of the gorgeous islands of Thailand. In the middle of a Wisconsin winter, a group of missionaries invited me to speak at their annual retreat in northern Thailand, so I leveraged the opportunity to take my bride on a mini vacation. And we brought back a bookmark to make sure we would never forget the "This!"

The boutique resort we found had a tiny stretch of private beach, protected on one side by massive flat-topped rocks. On top of the rocks were cozy couches that the staff set up every morning. That is where Kim and I would go to kick off our sandals, read books, and spend our days.

I must have gathered a year's worth of "This!" experiences during those few days—the rhythmic crashing of the waves, the warm sun in February (a lifesaver for a Wisconsite!), the schedule that only included eating, reading, and napping in various combinations.

We spotted an army of baby crabs marching across one of the rocks. We warmly welcomed the waiters offering fruit skewers and complimentary snacks. We watched the sun go down and struggled

---

* I just lost a bit of your respect just now, didn't I? Well, good thing I'm hanging out in the refuge of GOD's presence!

to leave the comfy couch in one of the most beautiful places we had seen on this planet.

"Can you believe we are here?" our smiles said to each other.

So when the wind chill is six below and the flannel sheets are the only thing keeping my scrawny body from hypothermia, I pull out the bookmark and stare at the picture of those flat-top rocks.

Better Than Our Best

Whether you have experienced the island life or not, I bet you have visited some beautiful places like the explorable forest behind your friend's house, the city park with the century-old trees, the cabin on the lake where the sun colors the horizon, the all-inclusive Mexican resort, the mountains after a fresh snowfall. You've felt the awe, warmth, and wonder of our planet's best places.

Which is why you should drool when you hear the words of Psalm 84: "How lovely is your dwelling place, LORD Almighty! My soul yearns, even faints, for the courts of the LORD; my heart and my flesh cry out for the living God. . . . Better is one day in your courts than a thousand elsewhere" (vv. 1–2, 10).

Than a thousand elsewhere?! One day with GOD is better than a thousand Koh Samui days, better than a thousand friends and family days, better than a thousand anywhere days.

Do the happiness math. How happy would you be if you could handpick the places where you would spend the next thousand days on this earth? How happy would you be if the next three years were spent traveling the world and taking Instagram-worthy snapshots of its cities, their human ingenuity, and GOD's natural beauty?

The answer: Not as happy as you would be after *one day* with GOD.

Like the psalmist, my soul indeed yearns for a place like that, nearly faints at the thought of being somewhere that stunning. Seriously, how good must it feel to stand in the very place where GOD is?

No wonder the Bible is filled with ways to talk about the places where "GOD is here!" All those references to GOD's house or GOD's temple or GOD's table or GOD's courts or GOD's kingdom or GOD's pasture or GOD's family are reminders of the greatest desire of our souls. They imply that GOD is here. This is why the simple promise "I am with you" or the name *Immanuel* (Hebrew for "GOD with us") meant everything to the biblical authors. They sought and saw GOD and believed that he is better than vacation destinations.

They believed GOD's presence is better than our best.

Makes your soul salivate a bit, doesn't it?

But that begs a life-or-death question upon which the Bible's best promises all hang: Can a person like you be in the place where GOD is? After everything we have done, is the door to the refuge open to people like us?

A False Assumption?

Up to this point, this book might have been based on a false assumption. I have been speaking to you as if you were a person who could stand in the presence of GOD. My words have implied that GOD accepts you, approves of you, and invites you to his table. I've made the thrilling claim that GOD likes you, that his face lights up when he thinks about you, and that the door to the refuge is open to you.

But that may not be true.

I promised in the opening pages of this book that this would not be a warm, fuzzy, vaguely spiritual book that avoids the stuff that Jesus talked about all the time—sin, the gnashing of frustrated teeth, and the reality of a horrific place called hell.

So, this is the time for us to talk to one another bluntly. Can a person like you be with a GOD like that? Can you look at yourself in the mirror and confidently say, "GOD is here!"? If so, can you prove it with more than just your personal opinion?

In other words, is this glorious, holy, wonderful GOD here with you or only over there with them?

Sin Turns Here into There

The very morning I wrote these words, I witnessed why we must not assume that GOD is here with everyone on earth. Because I read her nonverbals.

As I was thinking about GOD, I heard a blaring shout with enough decibels to penetrate my office window. I saw, walking down the sidewalk outside our church, a young couple in the midst of an argument. While I couldn't make out the point of contention, I could tell the guy was furious. Scowling. Gesturing. Vomiting out words.

She, on the other hand, was silent. Arms crossed. Head down. Unresponsive.

Most important, she was walking away as he planted his feet on a square of sidewalk concrete. As he stood, she separated. Her pace quickened, and the distance between them grew. Soon she was out of sight. Frustrated, the young man turned his back and walked in the other direction.

While I don't know what happened on the sidewalk, I would bet my best Bible that sin was involved. Some selfish, unloving, win-at-all-costs words. Maybe an insulting name or an exaggerated claim. Maybe a bloated opinion or a rehashing of her past wrongs. But while I am not sure of his sin, I did see its effect.

Separation.

Because that is what sin does. Whenever we replace love with sin, it separates people. Like the force between two repelling magnets, sin pushes us apart so that the person who was once right here ends up over there.

You have experienced this, right?

Maybe your dad was overbearing and verbally abusive. Maybe he self-medicated his loneliness with a six-pack of Pabst and took out his unsatisfied soul on you. And what did his sin do? Made you want to run away. Made you hide in your room. Made you long for a reason to get out of the house.

Because sin separates.

Your best friend in high school broke your trust. You thought you could tell her anything, so you did. But one day, desperate for attention from someone she admired, your friend betrayed you. And what did her sin do? Made you want to avoid her locker. Made you find a new place to sit at lunch. Made you look for a new ride home after school.

Because sin separates.

You got into it with someone at church. A meeting of Christians got rather unchristian. Love got lost in a battle of strong wills. Stuff got said that broke the hearts of the eavesdropping angels. And what did all that sin do? Made you want the meeting to end. Made you avoid the next Sunday handshake. Made you think about finding a new church.

Because sin separates.

This is what sin always does. Sin is the splitting maul that breaks apart the unity of GOD's people. It drives a wedge and pushes people from a peaceful here to a hostile there.

It drives a wedge between us and the GOD who is here.

Sin Separates Us from GOD

The biblical authors declare that sin has the same effect on our invisible relationship with GOD as it does on our visible relationships with people.

Isaiah explained, "But your iniquities have separated you from your God; your sins have hidden his face from you, so that he will not hear" (Isaiah 59:2).

Sins cross out the theme of this book, pushing GOD away so that he is *not* here. They are offensive enough that GOD has to look away, hide his face, and ignore the very sound of our voice.

The prophet Ezekiel agrees, "The one who sins is the one who will die" (Ezekiel 18:4).

Death, in the biblical sense, is a separation. When you physically die, body separates from soul. When you spiritually die, soul separates from GOD. And the cause of this spiritual death is sin.

Paul, the guy who gushed about GOD's bottomless love, said the same thing to the Christians in Rome: "For the wages of sin is death" (Romans 6:23).

Wages are what you earn for your work. So if your work has been the thoughts, words, actions, or inactions of sin, you have earned death and separation from the glorious place where GOD is.

But wait. Is that really true for all sins? I mean, I don't know you personally. You might be a morally solid person. Not perfect, of course, but a genuinely good, thoughtful, trying-your-best human being. Are Isaiah, Ezekiel, and Paul really saying that anyone who doesn't live a sinless life deserves to be separated from GOD?

Before I tell you how Paul answered that question, let me give you two things to think about: a court date and a dinner date.

Imagine you are sitting in court with the man who killed your best friend in a tragic drunk-driving accident. After a few birthday shots, this man got behind the wheel, drifted over the yellow line, and left your best friend's mother grieving for the rest of her life.

But the defendant's lawyer stands up and tries to reason with the judge. "Your Honor, my client is a good man. He has spent fifty-three years on this earth and has only driven while intoxicated on one occasion. One single night. That means that, since his sixteenth birthday, he has driven sober 13,504 days and driven drunk just once. By my math, he has been a good driver 99.99 percent of his life. And, Your Honor, my client has never once robbed a bank or abused a child or committed a hate crime. He has kept 99 percent of this nation's laws 100 percent of the time. Therefore, I believe it is obvious he is a good person who does not deserve to be punished in any way."

How would you feel about that defense? I bet you would be furious. Because you're not looking for percentages or averages. You're looking for justice. You care about the one night, the one choice, the one sin that separated your friend from his family.

Get my point? GOD is not concerned about your moral batting average. As a GOD of constant love, he can't stand it when people aren't loved. Even once.

But hold up. Vehicular homicide is pretty serious. Isn't that analogy unfair for the vast majority of us who have never sinned in ways as serious as that?

Well, before we minimize our sins, maybe we should interview those we have sinned against. Try telling those people what a deserving person you are, and I bet they would respond the same way you did to that lawyer. They wouldn't care about your average morality or how you treat most people. No, they would feel deeply wounded by the one thing you said (or didn't say), the one way you treated them, the one rumor you started, the one flirtatious relationship you didn't stop, the one game when you took a cheap shot, the one time they needed you and you were too busy.

It only takes one sin to separate.

Not convinced your situation with GOD is that serious? Then let me take you from the court date to a dinner date.

Imagine that you are having dinner with the woman you claim to love. But you are frustrated with a situation at work, and all of her listening, compassion, and look-on-the-bright-sides aren't snapping you out of your Friday-night funk.

So, she reaches across the table, wraps her warm hands around yours, and encourages you, "Baby, no matter what happens at work, I will always be here with you."

To which you reply, "But I don't want you. I want my co-workers to like me."

At which the passing waitress stops, dessert menus in hand, and gasps, "Oh no you didn't!"

Can you imagine your lover's reaction? Can you imagine how the rest of dinner would go? The rest of your night? Unless you owned the ugliness of that comment, could the relationship even survive something so foul? Imagine if you flat-out said, "You're nice and all, but I need something more. You are not enough to make me happy."

But that's what every one of your sins says to GOD.

"GOD, your approval wasn't enough for me, so I had to get drunk with the football team to get them to accept me." "GOD, no matter what you claim about my worth, I am not someone unless I have the best grades, the best stats, the best family, so I have no time to read your Word or talk to you in prayer or go to church." "GOD, of course I'm worried. If I can't get a date or a promotion, all I will have left is you, and what good would that be?" "GOD, if I don't push to get my way, I might lose the outcome I need to have peace, which isn't being with you." "GOD, if I denied these urges that feel as natural as breathing, I would have to live eighty years with only you to keep me happy. And you're obviously not good enough for that."

Disgusting, isn't it?

That is why every sin separates us from GOD.

Every sin is a cosmic insult. It's a slap in the face of our heavenly Father. It's a misuse of his name; it's thinking so little of him and so much of everything else.

In one of the Bible's most humbling descriptions of sin, Paul explains, "For although they knew God, they neither glorified him as God nor gave thanks to him. . . . They exchanged the truth about God for a lie, and worshiped and served created things rather than the Creator—who is forever praised" (Romans 1:21, 25).

The heart of sin is a refusal to glorify GOD as GOD, an absurd claim that GOD is not a big deal. It's a gruesome exchange where temporary, created things are given the highest worth and the eternal Creator GOD is ignored by ungrateful souls. Paul knows GOD deserves to be forever praised. But sin silences praise and saves its worship for the things of this world.

Author Jackie Hill Perry adds, "Unbelief will always contrast sin with God. Making *it* and not Him glorious."[1]

You will never see how serious your sin is until you grasp the glory of GOD. Punch some loudmouth, trash-talking barfly in the face and no one will think you are that bad. But throw the same punch into the face of your father who has sacrificed decades of time and thousands of dollars for you, and everyone will think differently.

Same sin. Different one sinned against. Which makes any "small" sin big enough for GOD to turn his face away like that offended woman outside my window. His holiness makes every sin serious.

Including mine. And yours.

Prostitutes, Goats, and GOD

This was the main point of a famous story Jesus told to the crowd of hookers and holier-than-thou-ers gathered around him. In Luke 15, Jesus made up a tale about a loving father, a wild son, and an obedient older brother, but the moral of the story is easy to miss unless you are thinking about the presence of GOD.

The story starts with the absurd request of the second-born son. "The younger [son] said to his father, 'Father, give me my share of the estate.' So he divided his property between them. Not long after that, the younger son got together all he had, set off for a distant country and there squandered his wealth in wild living" (Luke 15:12–13).

That "wild living" included a lifestyle that made *The Hangover* look like *Mary Poppins*. This ungrateful son took his father's hard-earned money and blew it on whores and Heinekens.

But notice the detail in Jesus' description: The son "set off for a distant country." He separated himself from his father. He slapped him in the face and said, "Dad, being with you isn't enough for me. I need more than you to be happy. I want to leave your presence here and do life over there."

Thankfully, the kid eventually realized how wicked he was. He confessed his sin and expected the consequence of being separated from his father's dinner table, but the dad memorably messed with his son's mind when he decided to forgive, accept, and throw a party to celebrate his return. "You can sit right here with me," the gracious father said.

But the older brother was not in the celebrating mood. "The older brother became angry and refused to go in. So his father went out and pleaded with him. But he answered his father, 'Look! All these years I've been slaving for you and never disobeyed your orders. Yet you never gave me even a young goat so I could celebrate with my friends. But when this son of yours who has squandered your property with prostitutes comes home, you kill the fattened calf for him!' 'My son,' the father said, 'you are always with me, and everything I have is yours'" (Luke 15:28–31).

Did you catch it? The father's response to his bitter son was, "You are always with me." Unlike his foolish younger brother, this son spent every day in his father's presence.

But, apparently, what he really wanted was a young goat.

Yep. A goat.

Jesus' story is fascinating, because it proves we all, at the heart of the matter, have the same spiritual struggle. We are not content to just be with GOD. His presence doesn't satisfy us. We either rebel and run off in reckless living or we get really religious, grudgingly obeying but secretly stewing about the "young goats" we never get.

But both lifestyles are supremely offensive. Because they both imply that GOD is not enough to make us happy.

Good People Die in GOD's Presence

Even if you don't consider yourself a rebellious prodigal or an ungrateful prude, you still have a separation issue with GOD. This is what even the "good people" in the Bible discovered.

On a few rare occasions, GOD revealed his glorious holiness to human beings like Isaiah, Peter, and John. These were not the spiritual hypocrites of the day, but the guys who sincerely cared about their beliefs and behavior. These were people who tried, who comparatively kept the rules and loved their neighbors. But being that good wasn't good enough to be with GOD.

Look at what Isaiah confessed: "In the year that King Uzziah died, I saw the LORD, high and exalted, seated on a throne; and the train of his robe filled the temple. . . . 'Woe to me!' I cried. 'I am ruined! For I am a man of unclean lips, and I live among a people of unclean lips, and my eyes have seen the King, the LORD Almighty'" (Isaiah 6:1, 5).

In an instant, Isaiah knew his lips were as unclean as the juiciest gossips' and foulest slanderers' among his people. He couldn't stand to stand next to GOD.

Peter admitted the same thing. Luke 5:8 records what happened when Jesus revealed his glory and proved he was GOD in human flesh: "When Simon Peter saw this, he fell at Jesus' knees and said, 'Go away from me, Lord; I am a sinful man!'"

Peter was not a child abuser, but he realized that he didn't belong in the same boat as GOD. The Light of the World instantly exposed the dark parts of his heart. And his shame begged Jesus to go away from "here."

Which was John's experience too. In the final book of the Bible, John suddenly saw the glorious face of Jesus, no longer hidden in humble form. "I turned around to see the voice that was speaking to me. . . . His face was like the sun shining in all its brilliance. When I saw him, I fell at his feet as though dead" (Revelation 1:12, 16–17).

Dead. The guy who was Jesus' best friend on earth nearly dropped dead when he saw him in his heavenly glory.

These "holy men" realized GOD was holier than they had ever imagined. Like tourists at the edge of the Grand Canyon, the closer they got to GOD, the more threatened their standing became. And they instinctively stepped back to a safer distance.

So, if you ever say to yourself, "I'll be with GOD when I die. I'm a pretty good person," consider your morality next to that of Saint John, the apostle of love. Maybe being good isn't quite good enough.

Isaiah, Peter, and John can tell you. Sin, any sin, will kill your confidence. Any mistaken belief that you are good enough will disappear when you actually see GOD as he is.

In other words, no matter who you are or what you have done, we are all in the same sad situation. Without divine help, none of us can claim, "GOD is here!"

About Heaven and Hell

In a culture that fills heaven with DMV lines, standard-issue diapers, and grown men with harps, missing out on heaven might not seem all that serious. And when hell appears to be the place where people sin (which can be pretty fun), maybe hell seems like a preferable destination. But a firm grasp on GOD should clear up all those cultural rumors. Let me start with some simple definitions:

Heaven = GOD is here in the fullness of his love and glory. Hell = GOD isn't here at all.

My definitions for heaven and hell come from Jesus himself. In the hour before his death, Jesus said to the sinner at his side, "Truly I tell you, today you will be with me in paradise" (Luke 23:43). Where would this man go on the very day of his death? To paradise, to heaven, the place where GOD is.

Compare that to Jesus' chilling descriptions of hell. While we often obsess over the imagery of fire and darkness, the essence of hell is the absence of GOD's presence. "Then [the King] will say to those on his left, 'Depart from me, you who are cursed, into the eternal fire prepared for the devil and his angels'" (Matthew 25:41).

Depart from me. Go away. You cannot stay in the place where GOD is. Hell is only dark because it is so far from the GOD who is light. Hell is described as being filled with fire, because when your hand touches the flame, you forget about everything in life except that pain. Hell is what we feel when GOD is completely gone.

158

There is no "This!" in hell. There is no happiness or laughter or friendship or safety or acceptance or love or family or compassion or warmth or inclusion. There are no parties or celebrations or vacations. Anything that makes you feel joyful or hopeful or peaceful or grateful is gone. And, since GOD will never make a guest appearance in hell, those emotions will never return. There is only weeping and gnashing of teeth at the horrific thought that you will never get a glimpse of GOD again.

While we live on earth, we—even those who reject GOD entirely—can experience the warmth and light and life of the sun. But hell is like being on a distant planet where life, in all of its beauty and comfort, cannot exist.

Why Hell Is Hell

Which makes your spiritual standing with GOD the most important issue of your entire life. No wonder Jesus said, "What good is it for someone to gain the whole world, yet forfeit their soul?" (Mark 8:36). What good would it be to gain one hundred years' worth of earth's best "This!" moments and then spend one hundred million years This-less?

None at all—because hell is much more serious than it seems.

You Would Make Heaven Hevel

Allow me one final sobering point before sharing some desperately good news. GOD has to take your sin that seriously, because allowing you into heaven just as you are would make heaven hevel.

All the peace and joy and relaxation of heaven would disappear like a puff of car exhaust if GOD allowed you into his presence as is.

This would never happen, of course, since GOD's glory protects the happiness of everyone around him, but for a moment, let's try this thought experiment. Imagine if GOD allowed sin into heaven.

You might only be a slightly impatient or an occasionally unkind person, but the words "slightly" and "occasionally" imply that you might sin against me at any time. How could I truly have peace if a person like you were walking around in paradise? You might only get angry in certain circumstances or say ugly things when pushed into a corner, but that means that my eternity could be filled with your anger or the echo of the ugly things you said.

In other words, what would a person like you do to heaven?

By comparison to the criminals in my city, I am a good person. But those who live in my presence know that I don't always bring joy. Sometimes, I take it. GOD knows I take it all too often. . . .

In other words, a person like me would make heaven a not-so-better place.

This is why the Bible's final paragraphs include these words: "Blessed are those who . . . go through the gates into the city. Outside are the dogs, those who practice magic arts, the sexually immoral, the murderers, the idolaters and everyone who loves and practices falsehood" (Revelation 22:14–15).

Everyone who practices falsehood. Everyone who doesn't live by the truth. Everyone who isn't washed and clean and holy cannot walk into the holy presence of GOD.

Which is why we need someone to wash us clean and make us holy.

Which is why we all need Jesus.

Jesus is the Savior who makes our sentence true. He is the only one who never diminished GOD yet also offered access to his here-ness.

That's the Jesus we meet in the pages of the Bible.

The Right Jesus

There are lots of Jesuses out there.

Some of my soccer teammates tell me Jesus is GOD or a prophet from GOD or a conversation starter or a conversation ender. Netflix shows inform me Jesus was the Son of GOD or just an influential rabbi or a figment of our religious imagination. The rumor mill says Jesus is our teacher or our example or our homeboy* or a thousand other curious, but entirely unimpressive, versions.

But for GOD to be here, only the right Jesus will work.

Turn GOD into a try-your-hardest God or a neutered-and-never-mad-about-sin god, and any kind of Jesus will do. But once you believe in GOD, you need the real Jesus, who can deal with your separating sin in order to welcome you into the one place that is better than a thousand days elsewhere.

This is the Jesus the Scriptures describe—the Jesus who lived, died, and rose in order to make it possible for every true Christian to shout, "GOD is here!"

Jesus Lived

You may be aware that Jesus lived a thirty-three-year-long life on earth about two thousand years ago. He was born in Bethlehem and raised in Nazareth, and he spent a few holy-day vacations in Jerusalem. But you may not realize that Jesus never once gave GOD a reason to distance himself over "there."

Jesus loved GOD perfectly, with all of his heart. Jesus never replaced GOD as his greatest treasure or closest friend. Jesus thought the world of GOD and couldn't stop talking about GOD's name, GOD's glory, and GOD's love. Jesus remembered the Sabbath and rested from his work to prove his trust in GOD's promise to provide. Jesus honored his mother and stepfather, even though he

---

* I believe Britney Spears once wore a T-shirt picturing this type of Jesus. To me, he didn't look much like GOD.

was literally holier-than-them, because his joy was in GOD and not getting his teenage way. Jesus never murdered, not with his hands or even with the thoughts of his heart, because his strength was in GOD, not in putting his critics in their place. Jesus never flirted with a married woman or gave in to a lustful look, because being with GOD provided more pleasure than sex ever could. Jesus was generous with his time and never stole a single tool from Joseph's job site, because his daily dialogue with GOD made him rich. Jesus never lied about anyone or exaggerated to win an argument, because he knew the truth about who and where GOD was. Jesus never coveted and was always content, because no matter what GOD took away, it was never his glorious presence.

Jesus never sinned. His love and purity and humility weren't hevel; they weren't here today and tomorrow dissolved into thin air. The always and nevers of GOD's presence applied to Jesus' obedience. He always sought and saw GOD. He never stopped doing what was best for the people around him.

Even his enemies admitted it with frustration. When they put him on trial, they rummaged through the robes in his closet and examined every used sandal, hoping to find the dirt of places Jesus shouldn't have been or the scent of a woman he claimed to have never met. But they couldn't. Because Jesus never sinned. The author of Hebrews stated, "We have one [that is, Jesus] who has been tempted in every way, just as we are—yet he did not sin" (Hebrews 4:15).

The sinlessness of Jesus is stunning. Can you even imagine going a week without worry or wanting to smack sense into the stupid people in your life? But that's what Jesus did. Can you fathom not just obeying, but wanting to obey, every single command in the Scriptures, even the ones about forgiving for the seventy-seventh time and turning the other cheek? Jesus always did. Can you picture a life where people are not annoying interruptions but opportunities for compassion? Jesus did.

He was a living example of "This!"—a glimpse of perfect truth and love walking the streets of Israel.

And since Jesus never sinned, he wasn't separated from GOD by even one degree. Instead, he lived in the glorious presence of GOD without averting his eyes or covering his face or begging for mercy. Unlike Peter, he never cried, "Lord, go away from me!" Unlike Isaiah, he never confessed, "I am a man of unclean lips." Instead, he rejoiced in the constant affirmation of his Father, the GOD who smiled down at Jesus' baptism and said, "This is my Son, whom I love; with him I am well pleased" (Matthew 3:17).

Imagine how much GOD loved his Son, Jesus! How pleased and proud he must have been when every single day Jesus loved GOD above all things, trusted him above all things, and honored him above all things.

I feel the same way about my girls when they make a beautiful choice, selflessly serving those around them with hard work and kind words. A dad can't help but smile when he sees the loving obedience of his kids.

Which meant GOD was always smiling at Jesus.

Jesus Died

Yet, despite being the world's perfect "This!", Jesus went through a grisly amount of "That."

He was separated from the approval and acceptance of humanity. Despite his unfailing love, they failed to love him and cried, "Crucify!" So they found a few nails and hung Jesus up to die.

But the exposed nerves from the nails and slow suffocation on the cross weren't the worst part. What tortured Jesus the most was the hour GOD turned his face away. After thirty-three years of "GOD is here," suddenly GOD wasn't. And Jesus screamed, "My God, my God, why have you forsaken me?" (Mark 15:34).

Forsaken. Abandoned. Alone.

On the cross Jesus went through hell.

Why would GOD do that to his perfect Son? Never mind the wicked men who voted for the cross, why would GOD join them in separating himself from Jesus? If sin is what separates a person from GOD, and if Jesus was himself sinless, why would GOD not be right there with him?

That might be the most vital question in human history. The entire mission of Jesus' life hangs upon its answer. So, why were those three famous words—GOD is here—temporarily not true?

The answer is . . . you.

Both GOD and Jesus knew you could not undo what you have done. No amount of mission trips or Red Cross donations could erase the separation earned by your sin. There would be no grading on a moral curve with GOD. You needed more than a second chance to not sin again. You needed a single payment to take away all your sins.

Jesus was exposed and abandoned on the cross so that the light of GOD's presence and the joy of GOD's people would be your eternal shelter and everlasting home. This was the wonderful trade Jesus made out of his unmatchable love for the world. "God made him who had no sin to be sin for us" (2 Corinthians 5:21). All the ugliness of our sin was put on the shoulders of Jesus, absorbed and endured by the sinless Son of God, so that all the beauty of Jesus' obedience would be wrapped around us for all of heaven to see and celebrate.

This is why Christians love the cross. The cross is not primarily an inspiring example of laying down our lives for other people. The cross is not a model for how to turn the other cheek. The cross is GOD turning the other cheek toward you.

Paul told the early Christians in Colossae, "[GOD] forgave us all our sins, having canceled the charge of our legal indebtedness, which stood against us and condemned us; he has taken it away, nailing it to the cross" (Colossians 2:13–14).

The divine charges against you, no matter how seemingly big or small from an earthly perspective, have been dropped. Cancelled. Nailed to the cross. The suffering of Jesus separated you from sin before your sin could separate you from him. And this is not some generic sin. This is the real stuff that you did. The real season of life when GOD seemed far from wonderful and worthy to you. The real arguments and compromises and clicks. The real stuff you hope your mother doesn't find out about. The real stuff you hope Google didn't record. That real sin, your actual sin, is what drove Jesus to pack his heavenly bags and come down to earth.

When you and I didn't earn it or deserve it, Jesus did it.

Jesus Rose

This kind of radical forgiveness seems impossible to us, so Jesus proved it by doing another impossible thing. He rose from the dead.

I don't mean he metaphorically rose in the thoughts and feelings of his former friends, "living on" in their hearts as they carried Jesus' teachings with them through life. No, I mean Jesus got up from the grave—skin and bones and lung-expanding breath. I mean he showed up to shock his grieving friends by showing them the wounds in his hands and in his side.

In the great resurrection chapter of the Bible, 1 Corinthians 15, the apostle Paul breaks out into an Easter song of praise, "The sting of death is sin, and the power of sin is the law. But thanks be to God! He gives us the victory through our Lord Jesus Christ" (1 Corinthians 15:56–57).

If Jesus paid the price for your sins on the cross, his resurrection from the dead was the cashed check. "In his great mercy [GOD] has given us new birth into a living hope through the resurrection of Jesus Christ from the dead" (1 Peter 1:3).

This is the source of our hope. The resurrection of Jesus from the dead is how you know, despite everything that has happened, that you have a for-sure future with GOD. Because GOD separated death from Jesus, life with GOD can never be separated from you.

GOD's Open-Concept Home

One of the most powerful pictures of Jesus' work was seen the day he died. It's described so briefly you might have missed it.

Here it is: "With a loud cry, Jesus breathed his last. The curtain of the temple was torn in two from top to bottom" (Mark 15:37–38). That might seem like a random mishap at the Jewish church next door to the cross. But it wasn't.

Back in the days of Moses, GOD gave very specific architectural directions for his temple. "Make a curtain of blue, purple and scarlet yarn and finely twisted linen, with cherubim woven into it by a skilled worker. . . . The curtain will separate the Holy Place from the Most Holy Place" (Exodus 26:31, 33). Cherubim are angels, spiritual beings who live where GOD is. Walk into the front room of the Jewish temple, and the entire design would signify that you were drawing closer to the place where angels live, the place where GOD is. Just behind the curtain, in some miraculous way, was GOD's very presence. In the Most Holy Place, people could meet with the Most Holy One.

But not just any kind of people. To enter a place that wonderful you had to be holy. King David wrote, "LORD, who may dwell in your sacred tent? . . . The one whose walk is blameless . . . whose tongue utters no slander, who does no wrong to a neighbor, and casts no slur on others" (Psalm 15:1–3). To get into GOD's sacred tent, you must be blameless. Which is why a thick curtain stood between sinful people and the sinless GOD. The temple curtain was a silent sermon that preached, "GOD is here, and you have to stay out there."

But then Jesus died and the curtain was torn from top to bottom.

Torn. Not pulled back for a quick peek. Not opened up for a one-day-only viewing special. *Ripped apart.*

From top to bottom. This curtain was six stories tall. If human beings tried to tear the fabric, they'd go bottom to top. But the destruction of the curtain wasn't the work of men and women.

This was the work of GOD. From top to bottom, he ripped apart the reasons for our separation.

And he did it all through Jesus! Jesus took our sins to the cross. Jesus deposited his wonderful life into our account. Jesus died for our sins and made a way for us to be with GOD.

On Good Friday, the Designer redesigned his church. He made heaven an open concept to all who turn their backs on sin and their faces toward Jesus. He tore down the walls between GOD and men, between sinners and saved.

This kind of gift compels us to respond. So don't stand back and just thank Jesus. Seek the face of GOD! Repent of your sins, trust in your Savior, and enter into GOD's presence! Because of the life, death, and resurrection of Jesus, every Christian has the right to walk right into GOD's presence.

STUDY QUESTIONS

1. Read Psalm 84. What connections do you see between this classic psalm and the concepts you have learned about?

2. Compare our cultural views of heaven and hell to the ways that Jesus described eternal life and eternal death. How might your life change if you embraced Jesus' definitions?

3. Explain this quote: "Every sin is a cosmic insult."

4. Why is the perfect life of Jesus just as important as the sacrificial death of Jesus?

5. Take a few moments to thank Jesus for the selfless love that allows you to enjoy GOD's presence.

CHAPTER NINE

What Most Christians Miss

Remember my presentation with Joy, the WWE teacher, and the metal safe where Joy found refuge? The day after I gave that message I got a very angry email written by a confused and frustrated sister in the faith.

"I couldn't believe what I was hearing," she wrote. "You told us that it's not all about the cross of Jesus. I never thought I would hear a pastor say that."

In her defense, I did say that. Hoping to get everyone's attention, I provocatively and intentionally said that I don't believe the Bible is primarily about the cross of Jesus. I don't think the final goal or end game of the Scriptures is for people to believe Jesus lived, died, and rose for them. I do believe those things are MASSIVELY* important, but I don't believe that's the true beauty of Christianity.

But, before you find the matches for a book burning, I should explain what I mean. Better yet, I should point to what Jesus himself said.

On the night before Jesus gave his life on the cross, he gathered his closest friends and told them, "I am the way and the truth and

---

* I left the caps lock on for that one, so you'd know how much I love the saving work of Jesus.

the life. No one comes to the Father except through me" (John 14:6). Beautiful, isn't it? Many Christians adore this verse because it is a vivid reminder that Jesus is supremely important for our faith. He is the only way, the source of absolute truth, and the key to eternal life.

But an equal number of Christians miss the greater point of that passage, namely, that Jesus is the way "to the Father." The entire reason he came to earth, lived, died, and rose was to get sinners back to the Father, into GOD's presence. Jesus' work on that holy weekend was not the end, but rather the means to a better end—GOD!

Think of Jesus' cross like the key to a beautiful home that GOD wants you to enter and enjoy.

Imagine if I found a homeless family on a February night in Chicago and gifted them the key to a spacious, cozy, fireplace-roaring, turkey-on-the-table home. Would I just want them to walk the streets and hold the key saying, "What a generous man Mike is!"? No, I'd want them to use the key to spend time inside the house!

GOD wants the same thing for you. Through the blood of Jesus, you have full access to the place that warms and fills your heart, the place where GOD is serving the spiritual food to satisfy your deepest longings for value and worth and acceptance. Jesus doesn't want you shivering and starving on the streets of this hevel world when the key to a better life is in your pocket.

Jesus wants more for you. He wants you to come to the Father to find life in his name, not just on the day of your death, but on every day of your life.

In the church I grew up in, we used to sing a short song about Jesus after every sermon. The lyrics were a paraphrase of a famous verse from John's gospel, a summary of what all twenty-one chapters of that book were about. The song went like this, "Hallelujah! Hallelujah! Hallelujah! These words are written that we may believe that Jesus is the Christ, the Son of God. Hallelujah! Hallelujah! Hallelujah!"

Solid, right?

But that's not all that John said.

169

Here's the entire verse: "But these are written that you may believe that Jesus is the Messiah, the Son of God, and that by believing you may have life in his name" (John 20:31).

Believing in Jesus is massively important to John, but it's not the end of his story. He wants you to be with GOD right now through the glorious name of Jesus. John wants you to enjoy the fact that GOD is here.

The author to the Hebrews echoes this, "Therefore, brothers and sisters, since we have confidence to enter the Most Holy Place by the blood of Jesus, by a new and living way opened for us through the curtain, that is, his body, and since we have a great priest over the house of God, let us draw near to God with a sincere heart and with the full assurance that faith brings" (Hebrews 10:19–22).

The author of Hebrews is all about the body and blood of Jesus, but he wants so much more for his friends—he wants them to draw near to GOD. We have confidence to do it! We have a way to get through the curtain into the most wonderful place of all! So let's do it now!

Through Jesus, the door is unlocked and wide open. Don't spend another day in a place of loneliness, rejection, shame, boredom, guilt, and hopelessness. Instead, draw near to GOD. Walk into the presence of the One who wants to be with you, already accepts you, is not ashamed of you, can excite you, has forgiven you, and has thrilling plans for you.

You already believe *in* Jesus, so now believe Jesus—go to the Father through faith in his Son. The door is open. The table is set. GOD is here!

The Point behind a Thousand Passages

So many of the biblical metaphors describing the work of Jesus are essentially about getting you into the presence of GOD. Christians might summarize the good news of the gospel with words like forgiveness or salvation or being justified, but those ideas are all spokes that lead to the hub of "GOD is here!"

Here are a few examples:

Jesus forgave you. To forgive, according to the Greek verb used in the New Testament, means to send something away. Therefore, Jesus' forgiveness means he sent all of your sins away when he died on the cross. Why does that matter? So that a sinless you could walk into the holy presence of GOD.

Jesus saved you. To save means to rescue someone from danger. Therefore, when Jesus saved you from your sins, he rescued you from a grave spiritual danger. Sins are so dangerous because they separate you from the presence of a perfect GOD. Jesus saves us from the danger of doubting our place in the presence of GOD.

Jesus justified you. To justify means to declare someone not guilty in a court of law. Jesus declared you justified when he rose from the grave on Easter morning. Why does that matter? Because guilty sinners are locked out of GOD's presence while the justified are free to walk out of court and be with GOD.

Jesus purified you. To purify means to remove the dirt and filth from someone or something. Jesus purified you by washing you clean of every sin. Why does that matter? Because only the pure in heart can, as Psalm 15 says, ascend to the holy place where GOD is.

Jesus redeemed you. To redeem means to pay a price to buy something back. Jesus paid the price of his holy blood to pay for your sins and buy you back. Why was that necessary? Unless you belonged to GOD, he would not take you home as his precious people to live with him forever.

Jesus sanctified you. To sanctify means to make something holy (wonderfully different). Jesus made you wonderfully different when he gave his perfect life to you as a gift. Why is that gift so good? Because now GOD can look at a perfect you and say, "Come here, kid! I love you!" instead of "Depart from me. I never knew you!"

Jesus reconciles you. To reconcile is to make peace between two previously hostile parties. Jesus made peace between a sinful you and a sin-allergic GOD when he died on the cross and rose from the grave. Why is the peace of reconciliation so important? Because it means that the doormat of heaven no longer reads, "No trespassing, sinner!" but "Welcome home, son!"

I could keep going, but I hope you get the point. The verbs of salvation are never the final blessing. Rather, they are gracious ways for you to get to the glorious end—GOD. The entire reason Jesus died and rose was so sinners could shout, "GOD is here!" GOD is what makes salvation worth celebrating.

The apostle Peter explained this when he wrote, "For Christ also suffered once for sins, the righteous for the unrighteous, to bring you to God" (1 Peter 3:18). Sinless Jesus suffered for sinners. Why? To bring you face-to-face with the face your heart longs for.

Even if you have been doing life your own way, Jesus forgave you so you could be with GOD. Even if there are years of addiction in your past, Jesus saved you so you could be with GOD. Even if you feel guilty and are guilty for what made your last marriage a mess, Jesus justified you so you could be with GOD. Even if you've lost count of your selfish thoughts or ungrateful days, Jesus redeemed you so you could be with GOD. Even if your foul mouth or backward priorities make you anything but morally wonderful, Jesus sanctified you so you could be with GOD. Even if you think all you've said and done could cause an entire church to burn down, Jesus reconciled you so you could be with GOD.

I'm not sure what bad things you've done or good things you've failed to do, but I am sure that Jesus never failed to avoid the bad and choose the good. And he did it all for you. To forgive you so completely you could confidently walk into the presence of GOD.

Friend, this is true. And it's for you too. Believe it. And you will have eternal life.

Eternal Life Proves the Point

Life, in the Bible, is all about being with GOD. If you recall, the word *death* means "a separation," so the word *life* points to "a union." If you have life with GOD, you are together with him. Or, GOD is here!

We've already defined *eternal* as something that "lasts forever," something that doesn't go to hevel sooner or later. So put together, the phrase *eternal life* means "to be with GOD forever." Unlike a celebrity meet and greet, where you get a handshake and a quick selfie, Jesus wants you to enjoy the presence of GOD for all eternity.

But here's the beautiful promise that I missed for most of my life: Eternal life starts now! The here-ness of GOD is not waiting for my final breath. It is as present as the breath presently in my lungs!

John's gospel, written by Jesus' closest friend, offers the best proof. The words *eternal life* are used seventeen times (40 percent of the Bible's total occurrences of that phrase), most often as something that has already begun for those who believe. Here are a few examples:

"Whoever believes in the Son *has* eternal life" (John 3:36, emphasis added).

"Very truly I tell you, whoever hears my word and believes him who sent me *has* eternal life and will not be judged but *has* crossed over from death to life" (John 5:24, emphasis added).

"Very truly I tell you, the one who believes *has* eternal life" (John 6:47, emphasis added).

You grammar lovers caught the verbs, didn't you? Jesus didn't promise that believers would eventually get eternal life at the ripe old age of seventy-six. He reminded them of the life that was already theirs, that had already begun when they first believed.

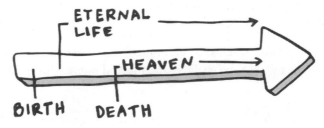

Eternal Life Starts Now

And what is that life? John answers that with a quote from Jesus himself, "Now this is eternal life: that they know you, the only true God, and Jesus Christ, whom you have sent" (John 17:3). True, satisfying, eternal life is knowing GOD. When you break up with the god of your past and embrace the GOD of the present and eternal future, you have discovered eternal life.

If you are a Christian, you are not sitting in a lifelong waiting room, counting the days until your eternal life begins. No, you have the same rights as GOD's own Son to seek him and see him, to be right with him, even today. Your eternal life starts now!

When "death" appears in your daily life and you are separated from something good, run to the life you already have with GOD. When your family rejects you, run to the GOD who accepts you. When your brother won't forgive you, run to the GOD who is overflowing with forgiveness. When another relationship doesn't make it, run to the GOD who always sticks around. When you let yourself down, run to the GOD whose work is flawless and whose commitment never wavers. When no one has time to actually listen to your struggles, run to the GOD who has all the time in the world. He is eternal, after all.

This is eternal life. A loving, kind, patient, selfless, gracious, powerful, wise, accepting, inviting, forgiving GOD who has left the door open for you to be with him today.

Through faith in Jesus, you already have eternal life. So live today knowing that GOD is here.

Every Spiritual Blessing, You Guys!

My friend Rebecca gets this.* I still remember the Bible study in my living room when she "acclaimed" Jesus, which, as you may recall, means that she enthusiastically and publicly praised him.

---

* Rebecca told me I could use her name only if I didn't give you the impression she's some kind of abnormally mature, above-average Christian, so I agreed to write this footnote. (But I think only an abnormally mature Christian would make me do that!)

She quoted Paul's words to the Ephesians, "Praise be to the God and Father of our Lord Jesus Christ, who has blessed us in the heavenly realms with every spiritual blessing in Christ" (Ephesians 1:3). Then Rebecca repeated those final words with vigorous hand motions, "Every. Spiritual. Blessing. You guys! Every. Spiritual. Blessing. That is awesome!"

Being her friends, of course we made fun of this eccentric behavior. But Rebecca was right. And, years later, her emotional reaction to that verse reminds me of what a big deal it is to know GOD through faith in GOD's Son.

Because of what Christ did, you have every spiritual blessing. Want love? You are loved by GOD himself. Want to be seen, known, and heard? You are, every time you pray to the GOD who loves the sound of your voice. Want someone to want you, choose you, include you? You are chosen by GOD, who wanted you in his family so badly that he went through hell to get you back. Pick a blessing, any spiritual blessing, and it is yours in Christ.

A few Christmases ago, two members of our church family, Dave and Rose, gave me a Christmas card. Inside was a generous check and a token holiday greeting from the card maker. Unlike most gift/card combinations, however, this time the message meant the most to me.* It read, "As you consider all the awesome things that have come to you through Jesus, remember that it is but a taste of all the good things that are yet to come."

Spot on. All the best parts about Christmas—the love of family, the invitation of friends, the generosity of others—are just a taste of the spiritual gifts that are yours in Christ. Christmas is actually a This-mas, a season filled with reminders of how amazing our GOD is and how everything is ours through faith in his incredible Son.

This is the life-changing power of the gospel of Jesus Christ.

---

* Does skimming the mass-produced sentiments every Christmas make me a bad person? Well, shoot. . . .

But how exactly is that truth life-changing? What does it look like to spend today aware that GOD is here?* Read on.

GOD Is Here: A Tutorial

Nothing gets my heart back to the eternal life that Jesus wants for me faster than repeating and reflecting on my favorite sentence—GOD is here.

Sometimes in my occupation I get critical emails. Some of them are well-deserved, rightful critiques of something I foolishly did or inadvertently said. Others are unfairly scathing and hard to forget. As much as I try to remember that everything is temporary, even people's approval, words can still hurt. It is too easy for me to put those emails in the Crock-Pot of my heart and let them simmer on low all day.

Ever been there? A classmate criticizes the way you look or laugh. A coach snaps, and your weaknesses echo off the walls of the gym. A significant other texts you a list of your wrongs to prove why *they* are right. It's hard to go more than a few days without hearing the words that hurt more than sticks or stones. But before we give up our joy and peace, let's not forget the words Jesus died to make true—GOD is here.

Here's how I do it—I close my email and look at the couch in my office, trying to envision GOD. Not a dopey god or an unapproachable God, but GOD in all his "caps lock" glory. There sits GOD the Father, and he's smiling at me, without an ounce of disapproval or disgust in his expression. After all, I am absolutely forgiven and, by the blood of Jesus, as pleasing to GOD as his perfect Son. Next to him is Jesus, GOD the Son, equally happy with me because of the scars in his hands and feet. And then there's GOD the Spirit, grinning and nodding toward the other two, reminding me how

---

* Do you ever get annoyed when authors pretend you're asking questions you never actually asked as a way to transition from one idea to another? I do too. I would never do that to you, faithful reader.

wonderful GOD is and how near I am to him because of what Jesus did.

After I look away from my laptop, I "look" at GOD. I talk with GOD and listen to him as I remember all that his Word says about me. I preach to my own heart, reminding it how glorious GOD is and how much GOD is for me. Since GOD is all-knowing, he is more than aware of my sin, yet he has chosen to send those sins away and treat me as I don't deserve.

That little habit works. Not every time, but much of the time, it works. Emotionally, his presence changes me. Seeking and seeing him in his compassionate glory gets to my heart in all the right ways. That is the power of those three words—GOD is here.

I do the same thing when I'm in a confusing funk. Some days, I discover a moody man behind the wheel of my minivan. No, the Town & Country was not carjacked by a depressed carjacker. That moody man is me. Sometimes I can't even explain why I'm not happy.

So, I run back to my favorite sentence. I glance over at the empty passenger seat and try to remember that GOD is here. I always picture him the same way—big smile, raised eyebrows, and that look that snaps me out of my moodiness.

In full disclosure, this habit isn't a magic bullet. Some days the joy doesn't come quickly. Or at all. Other days the fears and worries flood back into my mind as soon as I get back to my email or get my eyes back on the road. But even still, there is power in visualizing those three words.

Would you be willing to give it a try? When your failures to be perfect, or their failures to be perfect toward you, bruise your heart's happiness, stop, breathe, and see the GOD who is with you. He's riding shotgun. He's smiling in the rearview mirror. He's in the meeting room or on the factory floor or at the desk next to yours.

GOD is here. GOD delights in you.

And that fact can delight you.

Your Stairway to Heaven

In many ways, this eye-opening paradigm shift is what Jesus' ancestor Jacob experienced. One day, GOD opened Jacob's eyes to his divine presence, a moment that would alter the way this man looked at life on earth.

Do you know the story? Jacob was on the run from his angry twin brother, Esau. Jacob had just robbed him of the family blessing by impersonating Esau and duping their blind, elderly father.*

So Jacob took off to lie low with some distant family members until the rage evaporated from his brother's face. But as he lay down to sleep one night on the long journey from home, he found out a shocking truth: GOD is here.

> [Jacob] had a dream in which he saw a stairway resting on the earth, with its top reaching to heaven, and the angels of God were ascending and descending on it. There above it stood the LORD, and he said: "I am the LORD. . . . I am with you. . . . I will not leave you until I have done what I have promised you." When Jacob awoke from his sleep, he thought, "Surely the LORD is in this place, and I was not aware of it." He was afraid and said, "How awesome is this place! This is none other than the house of God; this is the gate of heaven."
>
> Genesis 28:12–13, 15–17

Jacob's lightbulb moment revealed that GOD is here. He didn't know it at first, but the random place where he spent the night was an awesome place because GOD was in it. And GOD promised that wherever Jacob traveled, he would not leave him but always be with him.

Heaven might seem far away, but there was a stairway, a connection between the GOD of heaven and GOD's people on earth.

---

* But, before we judge Jacob, who of us hasn't covered our arms in goatskins, imitated our twin brother's best stew recipe, and lied to our blind father in order to get our hands on the family blessing? #terribleapplicationpoint?

Jacob responded with amazement, "How awesome is this place!" Which is what you can say, even about the place where you are reading these words.

You might be lying on a mattress that is old enough to vote, but because of Jesus, that is an awesome place—GOD is with you!

You might be sitting at the doctor's office next to stacks of pop culture magazines and standard-issue waiting room chairs, but because of Jesus, that is an awesome place—GOD is with you!

You might be squeezed into your entry-level-job cubicle, but because of Jesus, that is an awesome place—GOD is with you!

You might be driving your rusted-out Honda Civic, but because of Jesus . . . wait, why are you reading this while driving, people?! Pull over before you hurt someone!

You might be pulled over in a gas station parking lot in your Honda Civic, but because of Jesus, that is an awesome place— GOD is with you!

No matter how bland or boring the place where you are, Jesus transforms your GPS location into a tourist attraction, because GOD is here. Perhaps you were not aware of that before this book, but now you know the most important truth in all the world— because of Jesus, GOD is here!

Three Words Down and a Blessing to Go

If you are like most modern people, your phone buzzed or beeped no fewer than 1,386 times during the time it took you to read this book. You probably ate multiple meals, took plenty of bathroom breaks, and made a few pit stops for sausage breakfast sandwiches.* So before we end our time together, let's do a quick review of the most important sentence in all of spirituality:

GOD—When you think of GOD, think of the most glorious, exciting, comforting, loving, peace-giving, happiness-increasing force on earth . . . then multiply it by a billion. GOD created a

---

* For which none of us blames you.

179

universe full of "This!", wonderful people and gorgeous places and memorable experiences, so that we could marvel at, honor, praise, adore, exalt, worship, fear, love, and think much, much, much more of GOD.

Is—Unlike everything in this world, which sometimes is but often isn't, GOD always is. He is not just the GOD of the past and future, but also of the present. He is eternal, everlasting, unfailing, faithful, constant, always with us, never forsaking us. Christians never have to worry about GOD disappearing like their breath on a cold day, because GOD is. This is our refuge and our strength, the place where we hide our hearts so that we can continually be joyful, peaceful, hopeful, grateful, and selfless people.

Here—A holy GOD can only be here with holy people. Since sin separates sinners from GOD, Jesus came into the world to put our sin over there so that we could draw near to GOD. Despite our daily spiritual struggles, those who trust in Jesus can boast of their present location, "GOD is here!"

Put those three words together and you have a powerful truth, one that can satisfy your soul and free you to serve others in selfless love.

My prayer is that our time together has opened your eyes to the glory of GOD and inspired your heart to seek his face until that unimaginable day when faith is no longer required and you see him with your own eyes.

And GOD's face will be shining upon you.

A Closing Blessing

Over the past few millennia, billions of believers have repeated and received the words of an ancient blessing, words that I would like to leave you with today.

They are words about GOD's desire to delight your soul and bless you. Words about the way GOD feels about you as his child and treasure. Words about GOD's persistent efforts to make you whole and give you peace.

Before I share those words, however, I want you to think about faces. When do people's faces light up at the sight of you? When do you look into one of those eyebrows-raised, eyes-shining, smile-beaming expressions?

Not with strangers. Walk through the mall and you'll find blank faces, bored faces, and strange faces. But not shining faces.

Not with enemies either. Some faces might know you, but the sins of the past produce scowls or wrinkles or narrowed eyes. But not shining faces.

No, a shining face requires two things—knowledge and delight. When I know you and delight in you, then my face lights up. When I am happy with my kids, they see a father's face that glows with approval. When favor and grace flavor the way I see you, then I can smile. And you can smile back.

Which is why this ancient blessing is so beautiful. So, brothers and sisters, go in peace today. Live with such satisfied hearts that you are freed to serve GOD with gladness. And receive his famous blessing: "The LORD bless you and keep you; the LORD make his face shine on you and be gracious to you; the LORD turn his face toward you and give you peace" (Numbers 6:24–26).

Because of Jesus, GOD blesses and keeps you.

Because of Jesus, our Lord is gracious to you and his face is always shining on you.

Because of Jesus, GOD is here!

Amen!

STUDY QUESTIONS

1. Do you agree or disagree with this statement: "Most Christians miss the main point of Jesus' suffering and death"? Why?

2. Read Ephesians 1:3–14. Write down at least six blessings that are yours in Jesus Christ.

3. Picture the face of GOD "shining on you" and "looking on you with favor" (Numbers 6). How might this mental picture help you through the challenging moments of the upcoming week?

4. Reflect back on all that you have just read. When this book goes back on your shelf, which ideas will you carry with you through the days to come?

Acknowledgments

Most people skip the acknowledgments page in the books they read, but you shouldn't. You never how many "This!" moments are waiting for you in the long list of names you don't recognize. More important, it is always good to remember how many great people GOD uses to create good books.

I would like to thank Asaph for writing Psalm 73, one of the best songs in human history. I'm not sure if you actually look like the picture in this book, but I hope you do, and I cannot wait to meet you in heaven.

A big shout-out to Mr. Bruce Eberle, the man GOD used to begin the process of this book. Without you, Bruce, I'm not sure if these words would have been written.

Kudos to Pastor Kyle Idleman. Kyle, we have never met, but the first time I read your humorous footnotes, I fell in love with your style. While I wish my fine print were as funny as yours, I'm grateful for your balance of humor and hard-hitting truth. I hope my attempt at the same comes close.

To the guy who invented the sausage breakfast sandwich, I love you. If you ever need someone to donate a kidney, I would do anything for you. Seriously. Anything.

Jason Jones from Jones Literary is exuberantly awesome. I'm not sure what exuberantly means, but it feels like the right adverb to celebrate the connection between ideas and talented people. Thank you.

Andy McGuire from Bethany House joined Jason in convincing me to hold on to those three words, even when I doubted whether anyone wanted to hear them. Thanks for putting courage in my heart, brother. I thank GOD for you.

Estee Zandee deserves a medal for her editing work. When my first draft came back with your 3,099 suggested changes, I may have forgotten about GOD's presence, but your careful eye and encouraging tone made this an amazing experience. (P.S. If "exuberantly" isn't the right word to describe how awesome someone is, let me know.)

To my friends who laughed out loud when they heard that I had more suggested changes to my first draft than Saint Peter had conversions at Pentecost, y'all are the worst. And I love you. Thanks for giving me so much "This!"

Bethany Vredeveld accepted the challenge of putting my ideas into pictures, and she knocked it out of the park. Bethany, you made abstract ideas concrete, fun, and, most important, clear. Asaph, I'm sure, will one day thank you for your amazing work.

I thank GOD for my church family at The CORE and two of my pastoral colleagues, Tim Glende and Michael Ewart, for allowing me the time to write. You gave me the space I needed to seek GOD and help others do the same.

To the mother of Hidekazu Tojo—Well done. On behalf of everyone who has enjoyed a California roll, thank you.

The Time of Grace team deserves pages of gratitude for their efforts and their support. Tim Lehman led the way to rally prayers and our team's individual strengths to make this book possible. I hope this work brings you joy as we attempt to bring joy to this world through Jesus.

Brooklyn and Maya, you have helped me experience a happiness that I didn't know existed before you were born. I have come to know our Father so much more since you entered my life.

To Kim, my bride, I'm staring at my laptop right now, trying to put twenty years of "This!" into a small paragraph, which is impossible. Thank you for listening patiently as I figured out GOD in my own head. Thank you for seeking GOD yourself. And thank you for forgiving me for all my bad jokes.

Finally, GOD, I want to thank you. For blessing me with all the people listed above and all the others unnamed. For filling the entire earth with your glory and then opening my eyes to it. Most important, for not being god or God, but the GOD who is always here with sinners like me.

Notes

Chapter 1: The Sentence That Can Change Your Life

1. A.W. Tozer, *And He Dwelt Among Us: Teachings from the Gospel of John*, comp. and ed. James L. Snyder (Bloomington, MN: Bethany House, 2014), 206–207.

Chapter 4: Two Unexpected Ways to Meet GOD

1. Paul David Tripp, *Suffering: Gospel Hope When Life Doesn't Make Sense* (Wheaton, IL: Crossway, 2018), 156.
2. Tripp, *Suffering*, 156.
3. Kathy Keller, "Don't Waste Your Sorrows" (presentation, National Day of Prayer Breakfast, Washington, DC, February 6, 2013).

Chapter 5: Hungry for Eternity

1. A.W. Tozer, *And He Dwelt Among Us: Teachings from the Gospel of John*, comp. and ed. James L. Snyder (Bloomington, MN: Bethany House, 2014), 24.
2. Augustine, *Confessions*, trans. Sarah Ruden (New York: Modern Library, 2017), 3.
3. The Rolling Stones, "(I Can't Get No) Satisfaction," on *Out of Our Heads*, ABKCO, 2002, compact disc.
4. Kendrick Lamar, "Sing About Me, I'm Dying of Thirst," on *Good Kid, M.A.A.D City*, Aftermath, 2012, compact disc.
5. *Midnight in Paris*, directed by Woody Allen (Culver City, CA: Sony Pictures, 2011), DVD.
6. Renée Elise Goldsberry with Lin-Manuel Miranda, "Satisfied," April 20, 2017, from *Hamilton: An American Musical*, video, https://www.youtube.com/watch?v=InupuylYdcY.

7. U2, "I Still Haven't Found What I'm Looking For," on *Rattle and Hum*, Island Records, 1988, compact disc.

8. Lynn Hirschberg, "The Misfit," *Vanity Fair*, April 1991, https://archive .vanityfair.com/article/1991/04/01/the-misfit.

9. Joshua A. Hicks and Clay Routledge, eds., *The Experience of Meaning in Life: Classical Perspectives, Emerging Themes, and Controversies* (New York: Springer, 2013), 333.

10. Trip Lee, "Why Fame Cannot Make You Happy," *Ask Pastor John*, Desiring God, May 13, 2015, https://www.desiringgod.org/interviews/why-fame-cannot -make-you-happy.

11. "Super Bowl 2019: 60 Minutes Looks Back at Tom Brady in 2005," *CBS News*, January 30, 2019, https://www.cbsnews.com/news/super-bowl-2019 -looking-back-at-tom-brady-in-2005-60-minutes/.

12. Bruno Mars, "Locked Out of Heaven," on *Unorthodox Jukebox*, Atlantic, 2012, compact disc.

13. Horace, *The First Book of the Satires of Horace* in *The Works of Horace*, trans. C. Smart, A.M. (Project Gutenberg, 2004), "Satire I," https://www.gutenberg .org/files/14020-h/14020-h.htm.

14. Timothy Keller, *Making Sense of God: An Invitation to the Skeptical* (New York: Viking, 2016), 88.

15. Foo Fighters, "All My Life," on *One by One*, RCA, 2002, compact disc.

16. Julie Bort, "'I've Never Felt More Isolated': The Man Who Sold Minecraft to Microsoft for $2.5 Billion Reveals the Empty Side of Success," *Business Insider*, August 29, 2015, https://www.businessinsider.com/minecraft-founder-feels -isolated-unhappy-2015-8.

17. C. S. Lewis, *The Weight of Glory: And Other Addresses* (New York: HarperCollins, 2001), 26.

18. *The Greatest Showman*, directed by Michael Gracey (Los Angeles: 20th Century Fox, 2017), DVD.

Chapter 6: Sad Symptoms of Putting Your Hope in Hevel

1. Jon Bon Jovi, "Always," on *Cross Road*, Mercury Records, 1994, compact disc.

2. Brian Johnson, "One Thing Remains," on *Be Lifted High*, Kingsway/Bethel, 2011, compact disc.

Chapter 7: Life in the Refuge

1. Bryan Chapell, *Unlimited Grace: The Heart Chemistry That Frees from Sin and Fuels the Christian Life* (Wheaton, IL: Crossway, 2016), 78.

Chapter 8: The Best "Here" We Ever Had

1. Jackie Hill Perry, *Gay Girl, Good God: The Story of Who I Was, and Who God Has Always Been* (Nashville: B&H Publishing Group, 2018), 152.

About the Author

Mike Novotny is a pastor, author, and unashamed lover of pop music and GOD (but not in that order). When not dating his wife and two daughters, Mike shares the good news of Jesus as the lead speaker of Time of Grace, a media ministry that engages with millions around the world each month. A lifelong soccer player, he was recently accused (by some millennial friends) of wearing shorts from the early 2000s that were embarrassingly short. But you shouldn't let that stop you from reading this life-changing book.